PERSONAL IDENTITY

Personal Identity

by C. H. ROLPH

London
MICHAEL JOSEPH

First published by
MICHAEL JOSEPH LTD
26 Bloomsbury Street,
London, W.C.1
1957

Set and printed in Great Britain by Tonbridge Printers Ltd,
Peach Hall Works, Tonbridge, Kent, in Times eleven on
thirteen point, on paper made by Henry Bruce at Currie,
Midlothian, and bound by James Burn at Esher, Surrey

CONTENTS

Odd that the passing of a thousand people—
Black paint flashing, black tyres hot on the road—
Should seem but a shadow in the train of one.
They fall past this still point like vacant seconds.

Have they not equal shares? It must be tyrannous
To watch un-moved, un-numbering, this protesting
Rush to non-entity; should we not flinch
From favourites who would leave the rest so little?

Tyrant, remember time; the enraged elders
Lift shaking hands to patient heaven, the poor
Play their trump cards for pity; sands already
Wait where your tomb will stand and could be honoured—

But no, no resolute virtue makes them live.
Their flat expressionless violence and great number
Ask for obliteration. They will seek vengeance.
Willingly theirs, no loss, when they can win.

'From a Window'
(G. J. WARNOCK)

ACKNOWLEDGEMENTS

I am very grateful to the following for permission to reproduce from their publications in the manner shown.

To Mr G. J. Warnock for his poem *From a Window*; to William Hodge & Co. Ltd, for various short quotations from their *Notable British Trials Series* and for a paragraph from *Finger Prints: History, Law and Romance*, by George Wilton Wilton; to Allen & Unwin Ltd, for a paragraph from Bertrand Russell's *Portraits from Memory*; to W. Green & Son Ltd., for two paragraphs from *The Scottish Police: An Outline of their Powers and Duties*, by James Mill; to the Controller of Her Majesty's Stationery Office, for extracts from *Hansard* about the case of Emery, Thompson, and Powers, and to the National Council for Civil Liberties for extracts from their Annual Report for 1956, about the same case; to Dr David Stafford-Clark and Penguin Books Ltd for an extract from *Psychiatry Today* (1952); and to the Hogarth Press for a paragraph from *The Dreadnought Hoax*, by Adrian Stephen. I am also beholden for many details of the Druce-Portland Case to Mr Theodore Besterman's book of that name published by Geoffrey Bles, and to *The Times* for the help always to be found in its impeccable law reports.

C.H.R.

I
IDENTITY
AS A LEGAL CONCEPTION

IN the eyes of Western law people become more individual, not less, as they become more numerous; the more we are together, the more separate we shall be. You can regard a modern registrar-general as the guardian of personal integrities or the instrument of a soulless collectivism, according to taste. Few of us, however, seem to know just what liberties we ourselves can take with the very personal mystery of our own selfhood, and in just what circumstances the law will allow us, as Hazlitt said, to 'lose our importunate, tormenting, everlasting personal identity and become the creature of the moment.'

The conception of the idea of identity, beginning as it does in early infancy, would have been lucky to escape the attention of the philosophers, but most of these have welcomed it as a means to the preservation of sanity. Locke, perhaps, did not help you and me very much when he called it 'the continuity of personal experience in the exercise of intelligent causal energy, the results being associated in memory.' We prefer the formula Smith = Smith. But it is true that most mental homes have at least one patient who alone knows himself to be Napoleon, Confucius, or Mr Danny Kaye, while complete loss of identity through amnesia is one of the most poignant of all the human tragedies; so that, whatever passing urgencies may suggest the need for temporary change, most of us cling anxiously enough to the idea of being, *faute de mieux,* ourselves.

Among the many reasons for wanting to be somebody

9

else, one must recognize the reasonable need for Kings to take holidays, actors to have unhistrionic intervals, stage and concert 'impersonators' to earn a living, schizophrenics to save up for their cures, and people dissatisfied with their sex to live as though they belonged to the other one. In this book there will be some consideration of this last group, the transvestists, who are breaking no law and often live lives of fear and misery because they think they are. But the book is concerned mainly with some victims of mistaken identity and unfounded accusation; with assertions of personality in the face of official steam-rollering; and with crooks—impersonators, frauds, impostors, false claimants, Hydes called up by Jekylls to exploit the mystery that clothes personal identity and ensures that, however closely society packs its individuals, you will always be able to see the joins.

In the past hundred years, Parliament itself has taken steps to protect numerous kinds of identity that confer special advantage or authority. There are various penalties for impersonating shareholders and stockholders, Chelsea pensioners, soldiers entitled to prize money or bounty or 'demob gratuity,' and voters at elections. You must not pretend to be an 'Inspector under the Factories Acts,' a policeman (except on the stage, where you can pretend as ludicrously or malevolently as the mood takes you and the producer permits), a soldier, sailor, or airman, whether for any nefarious purpose or for none, a 'prisoner's friend' willing to go bail, a Board of Trade agent on emigration duties, an Inland Revenue Officer seeking admission to premises, or anyone at all whose property (including land) you hope to get by your modest pretence to be someone else. The maximum penalties vary from life imprisonment for pretending to be a Chelsea pensioner, a pensionable soldier or his widow, a shareholder, or a person with rights to property, down to seven years for 'personating bail' and a

£50 fine for trying to get taken for a Board of Trade emigration agent.

There is, however, one kind of criminal impersonation that Parliament itself has never sought to punish, leaving it to the extensive resources of the Common Law; and this is 'personating a juror.' As the law stands at present, this is a misdemeanour punishable with imprisonment at the entire discretion of the court; another way of saying that the maximum is life imprisonment.

This seems to have been in some doubt (or, at least, there was a pretence that it was) until Mr Justice Avory in 1918 cleared the matter up at the end of a strange little story. Mr. Albert Foley, a farmer at Brentford, Middlesex, received an Old Bailey jury summons. He had two reasons for not wanting to be an Old Bailey juror: he was over the age limit (sixty), and he wanted to go to Devon on business. So on the opening day of the Old Bailey sessions he sent his farm manager, Francis Clark, to get him excused. Now Clark was known in and around Brentford as 'Mr Foley,' because here the social process of labelling and identity had fused master and man, as, in the case of a little-known farmer and his well-known bailiff, it often will. But Clark carried the thing too far. When his master's name was called in Court, he answered 'Here' and went into the jury-box, no doubt thinking that the time for explanations was not quite yet. But he took the oath, assisted in the trial of a prisoner for felony, and agreed on finding him guilty! The man gave notice of appeal, not because he knew about Mr Clark's impersonation in the jury-box but because he thought he had a good case for appeal anyway; and in the course of the next few days Mr Clark's guilty story reached his ears, upon which it must have fallen like a burst of uplifting music. He got a retrial (the Foley-Clark imbroglio having nullified the first one), and an acquittal. Then Mr Clark was indicted for the Common Law misdemeanour of impersonating a juror. A short legal argument

(in the Old Bailey again) established that this was in fact
and in law what he had committed, and left him no alternative but to plead guilty.

'I am satisfied,' Mr Justice Avory told him (and you can
imagine him twisting his cap as he listened), 'when you
were first called before me and admitted that you had
personated your employer, that you had no corrupt motive,
and that you went into the jury-box as you did in ignorance
that you were breaking the law. You did it under a kind of
blind obedience to the behests of your employer, as I
believe, but it may have been a pure misunderstanding.
Anyway I hope it will be understood in your neighbourhood
that you still bear the same character for integrity and
perfect honesty as you did before. It will be sufficient if
I fine you one shilling and order you to pay the costs of
the prosecution.'

Sufficient for Mr Clark, anyway, since the costs might
well have been £100. There is no record as to how the
Foley-Clark identity resolved its difficulty about the costs;
but the shilling fine was merciful, significant, and so far
as is recorded in the law books the only penalty for this
offence in living memory.

To anyone who has watched the process of summoning
and empanelling juries it is obvious that few kinds of
personation could be easier. If you agree to serve John
Brown's turn for him, you have merely to say 'Here' each
time his name is called in Court, and do all that is required
of him by the officials.

Symptomatic, though, of the law's respect for personality is its half-hearted insistence that the British citizen
shall identify himself openly. On the one hand, an army
of officials supports, and is supported by, this denial of the
right to perpetual *incognito*: income tax men, census men,
customs officials, scholarship bodies, the countless authorities that grant licences to do this or to be exempt from

doing that, and the police. On the other hand the police are often hamstrung by the right of the citizen to say 'find out!'

You cannot know all the cases in which the law is so determined to have your name and address that it authorises your arrest by the policeman to whom you refuse to declare them. In the great majority of cases a policeman who accuses you of committing an offence and then asks for your name and address is doing so because (a) he has no power to take you into custody or (b) he doesn't know whether he has nor not. In many of them you commit a further offence by refusing to give the required details, or by giving false ones; but even so, there are still many cases in which he cannot arrest you, and must follow you home if he wants to know where he can serve a summons on you. There are grounds for thinking that it would be against public policy to publish a list of these instances, public policy having come to rely so securely upon *ignorantia juris.* No list, therefore, follows.

There is not the same respect, in this as in most countries, for the personality of the visiting—or even of the resident— foreigner. If he stays here longer than three months he must carry an alien's registration certificate: if not, he must carry a passport (or some equivalent document) with a photograph in it. He must instantly produce any of these documents to any policeman or immigration officer who wants to see it. Unless its contents are false, therefore, his identity is an open book; he can have no *nom de guerre,* no secret life. And to change his name he requires, unlike a British citizen, special legal authority. (All this adds piquance to the certain knowledge that we always have in our midst a number of foreign visitors whose names, addresses, photographs, passports and pretensions are all false, who increase in numbers at times of international tension, and who have a way of forgetting who they are completely.)

*   *   *

Change of name, as part of the whole question of pseudonymity, merits a little attention here. Since the wartime identity cards were abolished in 1952 (an event described in Chapter II), it has been easier than ever to live quite lawfully under an assumed name. Not even the need for an identity card made it very difficult, for the card simply bore the name and address you gave to the Registrar, plus a number that would have been allocated to you whatever name you gave. This involved a little risk, which has since disappeared. You can now live under any name you like to adopt, or under any number of names. Some people use hundreds of names and order their lives by card-index. The effect of the law as to changed names is to make life more difficult unless the change is done properly.

'A man may assume any name he pleases in addition to or in substitution for his original name,' says *Halsbury's Laws of England,* meaning that he can do it without legal loss, keeping even his entitlement under any will, for example, that benefits him in the name he didn't like; 'and in adopting even the name or combination of names by which another person is already known he does not commit a legal wrong against that person. The law concerns itself only with the question whether he has in fact assumed and has come to be known by a name different from that by which he was originally known.'

So much for surnames. Because in the first instance they were arbitrarily assumed, so they can be changed at pleasure. Is there any difficulty about changing first names, an often innocent form of aesthetic rebellion amongst school-friends? *Halsbury* records, in almost obituary language, the canon law that allowed a baptismal Christian name to be changed at confirmation time, but *Halsbury* does not think an assumed Christian name is now any less valid than an assumed surname.

But people who change their names fall naturally into two legal classes. The smaller class does it for reasons which

the law deprecates and which the police, as they are intended to, find inconvenient. The larger does it for per-
missible purposes which the law will not obstruct or criticise
provided certain formalities are observed. You need to
'preserve testimony and obviate the doubt and confusion
which a changed name is likely to involve;' so you are
encouraged to do it by private Act of Parliament, by Royal
Licence, or by deed poll. The private Act of Parliament is
the grandest and most expensive of these, and now totally
unnecessary: the last time it was resorted to was in 1908.
A Royal licence *may* be necessary to comply with the terms
of a will and inherit in the name approved of by the
testator. You need to work out how much you are likely
to get under the will and compare the answer with the
figure (roughly £75) that a Royal licence will cost you in
stamp duties and other fees. If still so minded, you then
apply to the Home Secretary for the licence—which, it has
long been established, will not *give* the new name but merely
permit you to *take* it.

The best way is by deed, which costs little more than
£5 and still retains its ancient name of 'deed poll' because
it represents so simple an operation that it cannot afford
to shed one rag of verbal mystery. A deed is merely 'a
written instrument signed, sealed, and delivered.' Sealed,
today, means muttered over with the thumb pressed on to
a circular, adhesive red wafer the size of a sixpence.
Delivered, if it means anything, means deposited in the
Central Office of the High Court; and every deed is either
'poll' or 'indented.' If a deed is made by more than one
person, there ought generally to be as many copies of it as
there are parties to it; and because such deeds were formerly
laid together and cut or 'indented' in acute angles at the
top or side (the indentations thus corresponding with each
other), they are still known as indentures. Perhaps this
exactly repeated mutilation of two or more identical documents is one of the earliest known methods of safeguarding

the identity of inanimate things. There are unauthentic records of an ancient tribal custom of branding pairs of criminal conspirators with the two halves of a broken spearhead, but it has long been usual now to allow criminal *personal* identities to efface themselves with the passage of time.

In changing your name by deed poll, you must advertise your intention in a newspaper. And even if you change it without resort to any of these methods, advertising your new identity in a newspaper is nevertheless a sound precaution; years later, it may be, you will need evidence that there was in fact such a change, and the files of a newspaper have often been called upon to provide it.

Civilised society being in general what it is, and in particular what it thinks it is, one of the more recherché ways of changing 'identity' is to dress and live as a person of the opposite sex. This often involves complex psychological and emotional processes, and there seems to be no serious lack of books about these. Even if I lose sight of it every now and again, my own purpose here is to consider merely the attitude of the law to the numerous manifestations of human identity, in its accepted sense of the unity and persistence of the state of being a person.

To begin with, therefore, the law takes no notice of what the sexologists call transvestism. A man may live most of his life as a woman, or a woman as a man, without breaking any law. (It may become difficult at some time or other, through the need to fill up census papers, applications for licences, and statutory declarations of various kinds that are inquisitive about gender: but none of these matters affects the clothes you wear.) The popular belief to the contrary is strong, and derives in all probability from a Puritan past that considered it wrong to have any sex at all, let alone pretending to have the wrong one. The existence of such a popular fallacy might not matter much, and might even be justified by the minor beneficence that it induces people to dress reasonably, if it were not for the fact that there are people living in fear because of it. I have been assured by well-known surgeons that there are people of ambiguous sex who dare not go out because they do not know which dress to adopt, and who, even at home, live in needless terror of 'discovery' and prosecution. One of these surgeons himself believes this fear to be well-founded, and it will take much to shake him. I lately read the manuscript of a book by a prison governor who told the story of a girl sent to Borstal 'for two years' for 'living as a man.' It could not possibly be true: there must have been some offence of which the male dress was a concomitant—as, for example, in the well-known case of 'Colonel Barker,' who had lived as a man but who was punished only for making a false declaration, when she wanted to 'marry' another woman, to a registrar of births, deaths, and marriages. You cannot for long live openly as a person of the opposite sex without getting involved in the social conventions expressed in public notices like GENTLEMEN and, *a fortiori*, LADIES. There are, of course, men who dress as women in order to commit crime, or to attract and hold the attention of a policeman on his beat while other people commit crime. (This is sometimes easier than it ought to be, for beat duty can be lonely work, constables are often young, and abnormal biology is always interesting.)

But whereas it would appear to be a misdemeanour at Common Law to 'change the sex' of a normal patient by surgical operation, the law would be less likely to disapprove of an operation *conferring* or confirming sex in the case of a person whose gender was physiologically ambiguous. Such a drastic assumption of fresh identity, however, is not necessary in order to legalise the wearing of clothes appropriate to either sex. 'Masquerading,' as it is called by the people who think it should be punished, is perfectly lawful while it is done with circumspection.

All in all, the main principle to be kept in mind in considering the self as the subject or object of self-consciousness, and at the same time a conception of law, is that personal identity is proved in courts of law, not by reference to names, not even mainly by direct testimony, but 'presumptively' by evidence of similarities or differences in personal characteristics. And in criminal cases, though the evidence that seems to prove the deed may also prove its author, yet as a rule the proof of the two is separable. So it is relevant, and may be helpful, to prove motive or its absence, means or its absence, preparations or threats to do the deed—and the possession of any particular skill or qualification needed for it. As for the suspect's conduct *after* the deed, he can surprisingly often be relied upon to assist in his own identification by possessing property recently stolen, by fabricating or suppressing evidence too clumsily, or by running away. And here a word of caution may not be out of place: the suspect may be an innocent man, his 'conduct after the deed' may be conduct after someone else's deed. Take the case of Alan English, of Oldham, as reported in the *Daily Mirror* of February 16, 1956.

Alan English was deaf and dumb. When he was sixteen there occurred in his neighbourhood a series of pranks on women, especially in the village of Royton. Someone was going round the village late at night, knocking on doors and windows and then vanishing—choosing always a house where a woman was known to be alone for the evening. The angry men of Royton formed a committee of vigilantes, determined to catch the terrorist. On New Year's Eve, 1955, one of the vigilantes heard a knock on his front door. It was a woman living nearby, who had called to wish him a Happy New Year; but she ran back into her house after knocking, intending to give him a surprise when he came to the door. As he opened it he saw the figure of Alan English, a stranger to him, walking away in the shadows. He chased and caught him.

'What's your game?' he shouted at Alan. 'What are you doing?'

Totally at a loss, Alan tried to convey that he wished his new acquaintance a Happy New Year, hoping that that might prove to be the right conversational gambit. No words came, of course. He may even have seemed a little rude. So the vigilante struck him several times in the mouth, and he fell to the ground unconscious.

There was a prosecution for assault. 'This was a tragic and disastrous twist of fate to a well-meant plan', said the solicitor who defended the deeply remorseful vigilante. The Magistrates imposed a fine of £20. 'I can't find the words to say how sorry I am', said the defendant; 'it was a terrible tragedy'. And he had already given a warning to his fellow-vigilantes: 'Don't take the law into your own hands. I know now that a million-to-one mistake can be made—and end in terrible tragedy'.

The odds are not nearly so high. But let us turn to a consideration of some of the simpler methods by which personal identity may be proved beyond doubt.

II

IDENTITY CARDS

ONE November evening in 1950 Mr Clarence Henry Willcock, the general manager of a French dry-cleaning company, was sitting in a cab with his solicitor, Mr Lucien Fior. They were on their way to an election meeting at Uxbridge, where the Liberal Party were inviting the electors to have Mr Fior as their M.P., and Willcock, a lifelong Liberal, was to tell them why. 'You know,' said Willcock suddenly, 'I don't believe in identity cards.'

'Neither do I,' said Mr Fior. 'Nor Income Tax. Still, there they both are.'

'I think we could get rid of identity cards,' persisted Willcock. He thought it was an imposition that an entire population should be required to carry in its pockets and handbags this prescribed evidence of separate personality; he saw it as a challenge to the principles of individual freedom and integrity. To him, as to many other sturdy individualists, an identity card was an affront to human dignity, comparable to the brand on the flank of a sheep.

The war had been over for five years. The National Registration Act, 1939, had served its purpose. That purpose had been understood to be the compilation of a list of all our names and addresses, to facilitate the National Service call-up and the rationing of 'consumer goods' and to make life difficult for the Fifth Column. No one minded much in September, 1939. The immediate outlook was so much like the end of the world that people saw hope in every new

20

display of planning and authority. If they felt that their identities were getting lost in a vast uniformity of cardboard gas-mask boxes and Anderson shelters, they were also comforted to have their individuality reaffirmed with an official document on which one's number, at least, was different from anyone else's. And to make the scheme work, it was essential for Parliament to enact that anyone who failed or refused to produce his identity card to the police should be prosecuted and fined. The police were not empowered to arrest him, and it rather looked as though the power to do so had been deliberately withheld from them, for reasons still dimly associated with the liberty of the subject and the size of police stations. They did arrest, of course, whenever they thought it was a good idea; but when they did, if the episode leading to the arrest had seemed to have no other basis than the failure to show an identity card, it was surprising how often a further basis turned up.

Once the people had been allowed to get used to this new edict that they must not only be and stay one person, but prove if required that they were doing so, the screw was tightened considerably. A person who failed to produce his card was still guilty of an offence, though he could 'cure' it (and would not be prosecuted) if he produced it at a police station, which he could name to suit his own convenience, within two days; but he was now made liable, by way of a Defence Regulation, to further penalties if he refused to tell the policeman his sex, age, nationality, occupation, and whether he was married or single. Resentment grew.

In December, 1947, Mr W. S. Morrison, M.P., moved the annulment of the Regulation that required all this additional frankness in conversation with the police, and although that would still have left the original burden of identity cards intact, it was a way of forcing a debate about what he called 'these troublesome documents.'

'The main argument for them,' he said, 'is that as long as rationing persists they are necessary. I do not believe it. We were told in the House the other day that there are 20,000 deserters still at large. How have those 20,000 persons contrived to equip themselves with food and clothing? *Ex hypothesi* they cannot be possessed of valid identity cards, but that has not prevented them from sustaining themselves with food and clothing themselves with raiment. As a deterrent to the evasion of the rationing arrangements the case is proved: they are of little value.' At about the same time Sir William Darling told a London audience what he thought about identity cards. 'We should throw them on to the bonfire,' he said, 'and announce to the world that we have done so. We have become,' he added, 'a docile, dumb people, a nation of subservient cattle.'

A number of cattle wrote to the newspapers to say that they didn't really mind about identity cards. They pointed out that a lost pocket-wallet containing an identity card was more likely to find its way back to the owner; that tradesmen were more willing to accept a cheque if you showed your identity card; that the Post Office liked to see it when you pushed your bank-book under the grille; that people found unconscious in the street or suffering from loss of memory could by reason of their identity cards be the more quickly identified and returned to their friends. What was all the fuss about, asked one letter in *The Times*? 'To some,' it said, 'they seem to be one of the few wartime measures worth retaining . . . I foresee many citizens voluntarily carrying these cards, just as the foreign traveller used to provide himself with a passport when one was not required by law. In many ways they will be a safeguard to the individual as well as a valuable administrative adjunct.'

The adjuncts survived it all; and the police, who had by now got used to the exhilarating new belief that they could get anyone's name and address for the asking, went on calling for their production with increasing frequency.

If you picked up a fountain pen in the street and handed it
to a constable, he would ask to see your identity card in
order that he might record your name as that of an honest
citizen. You seldom carried it; and this meant that he had
to give you a little pencilled slip requiring you to produce
it at a police station within two days. You chose any police
station you liked.

A man came out of a cinema one evening with a lady
who was not his wife, and was stopped by a youth who
wanted a match to light his cigarette. 'I'm sorry,' said the
man, 'I'm a non-smoker.' The youth had been drinking. He
raised his voice about non-smokers and people who don't
like to be spoken to; the man became angry and a little
frightened; a couple of blows were exchanged, and two
policemen took the youth into custody for being drunk and
disorderly. 'Can you come to the police station, sir?' one
of them asked the man. 'Oh no, thanks.' (Don't want to be
mixed up in anything tonight of all nights.) 'Well, perhaps
you'll give me your name and address, please?' No, he
wouldn't do that either; he wanted nothing more to do with
it; goodnight. 'Just a moment sir: I'm afraid I'll have to see
your identity card.' He hadn't got his card in his pocket.
'Then I shall have to serve this notice on you to produce it
within a couple of days.' No, he just wasn't going to produce
it at all, anywhere.

Now, the policeman at this point must either let the man
go unscathed, thus incurring the anathema of his colleague
(who wanted a witness) and the displeasure of his superior
officers, or he must take him into custody. What for?
Assaulting the youth? Insulting behaviour? Disorderly
conduct? There must be something. He took him. At the
police station, not knowing whether the alternative was
going to be a night in the cells, the man gave his name and
address at long last, and was allowed to go home. A week
later he was summoned before a magistrate and fined ten

shillings for refusing his name and address to the constable, having first failed to produce his identity card.

Clarence Henry Willcock thought this kind of thing was an outrage.

'If I get myself prosecuted for not producing my identity card to a policeman,' he said to his solicitor in the cab, 'will you defend me?'

'Certainly,' said Mr Fior, and launched a cause célèbre.

A fortnight later, on the evening of December 7, 1950, Willcock was driving home to Barnet along Ballard's Lane, Finchley, at a speed which exceeded the thirty miles an hour permitted in built-up areas. He was stopped by P.C. Harold Muckle, and the formalities began. Car numbers, Road Fund licence, driving licence, certificate of insurance. Thank you sir. Identity card, please?

'No,' said Willcock firmly.

'You haven't got it with you?' said the constable.

'I didn't say so. I mean that I'm not going to produce it to you.'

Another constable came round the car. They both looked at him: you get all kinds, but they were not to know that this kind was the personification of liberalism with a small 'L' and a strenuous exemplar of what it is that keeps the fires burning so obstinately in Liberalism with a large one. A small man, Willcock was a great Liberal: he is remembered by a large number of people with affection and respect, to which, in the case of the London Liberal Party, there is added pride and the sense that he was peculiarly its property.

'Well, then,' said the constable, as he pulled a little wad of forms out of his notebook case, 'no doubt you'll produce it at a police station within the next forty-eight hours.' He began writing, on one of the forms, the name and address he had taken from the driving licence.

'I will not,' said Willcock.

The constable may have winced slightly, but he went on
writing.

'What police station?' he asked.

'No police station.'

'Now listen, sir——'

'You listen to me. I've got no complaint about you; no
doubt you're simply obeying instructions. I'm fed up with
these identity cards and the way you people are exploiting
an Act that ought to be dead and buried. I'm
determined——'

'I'll make it out for Finchley Station, sir. It's at 193,
Ballard's Lane, just up the road.'

'I tell you I'm not——'

'Maybe you'll be back this way in the morning? You
could drop it in then. Here you are, sir.'

Willcock took the form, screwed it up, and ceremoniously
tossed it into the road. The other constable tenderly
retrieved it, smoothed it out, and put it in the car. And after
a further exchange of prophecies about the identity card,
Willcock drove away.

Mr Lucien Fior received the summons a few days later.
The Middlesex Justices, sitting at Hornsey, were to try the
charge brought by Police Constable Harold Muckle that
Clarence Henry Willcock did fail to produce his National
Registration Identity card upon the demand of the said
Harold Muckle, a police constable in uniform.

Now Willcock and Mr Fior were old acquaintances; old
enough for the latter to be quite sure, when Willcock had
asked him if he would undertake the defence in such a
case, that the occasion was imminent. How could it be
fought? The facts were indisputable, they proclaimed themselves. If you fail to produce a document which the law
requires you to produce, a constable's allegation to that
effect throws the onus of proof upon you. It is thus with a
driving licence or a certificate of insurance (neither of

which, by the way, has ever seemed to arouse the ire of liberalism; the identity card system, by licensing a man merely to be himself, perhaps went just too far). Willcock was accepting no onus of proving that he did produce his identity card: he wanted a fuss made about the mere fact that he was required to do it at all.

The National Registration Act, 1939, was to endure 'for the period of the present emergency,' i.e., the second World War. The Defence Regulation that had sharpened it up and made it a bit more irksome, by enabling the police to ask you which sex you belonged to and whether you had ever got married, was being renewed every year by an annual Emergency Laws (Transitional Provisions) Bill. But if it could be shown that 'the period of the present emergency' had come to an end, then so had the Defence Regulation, which must die with it, and so had identity cards.

Now it happened that another important Act, the Courts (Emergency Powers) Act, which had authorised a large number of war-time aberrations in the administration of justice, had recently been 'terminated by Order in Council.' This Order declared that 'the emergency which was the occasion of the passing of this Act' had come to an end. In other words, the war was over. If, thought Mr Fior, it was over for one purpose, it was over for all. It was the same war, the same emergency. Therefore the National Registration Act was dead, and with it had died the obligation of the citizenry to own and carry identity cards, and the powers of the police to call for their production.

All this Mr Fior confidently urged upon the Magistrates, concluding with the submission that the summons against Clarence Henry Willcock was 'misconceived and disclosed no offence.' The Bench decided against him and convicted Willcock, but gave him what is called an 'absolute discharge' and agreed to 'state a case' for the consideration of the High Court. In the King's Bench Division, the appeal case of *Willcock v. Muckle* (1951, 49 L.G.R. 584), after a

preliminary skirmish before a court of three Judges, was
adjourned for argument by the Attorney General before a
full of court seven Judges because of the unexpected
magnitude of the issue it raised.

That issue was not merely the life or death of identity
cards, which had by now become a minor matter. If Mr
Fior's suggestion was right, and the 'end of the present
emergency' for the purposes of the Courts (Emergency
Powers) Act was also the end of the purposes of the National
Registration Act, then the same must be true of a large
number of other war-time statutes. They had all died
together—about thirty of them—and the effect on the
administration and commerce of the country would be
chaotic. Five of the Judges decided that the Courts
(Emergency Powers) Act had died alone—a decision, in
effect, that in thirty different Acts the words 'period of the
present emergency' could have thirty different meanings and
the war thirty different durations. That was the way it
seemed to Lord Goddard (the Lord Chief Justice), Lord
Justice Jenkins, Lord Justice Somervell, Mr Justice Hilbery,
and Mr Justice Lynskey. The remaining two Judges—Lord
Evershed (Master of the Rolls) and Mr Justice Devlin—
thought otherwise. The majority thus upheld Willcock's
conviction; but it is interesting that to this day there is a
large body of opinion among lawyers that Lord Evershed
and Mr Justice Devlin were right, that the issue was wrongly
decided; and when the case is discussed you will sometimes
hear it said that if some general statute, designed to clear
up the legislative débris of the war by scheduling thirty-
odd Acts of Parliament for repeal *en bloc,* had inadvertently
missed one out, the Judge might well have found that the
intention to repeal it must be presumed.

But Willcock's case was not to end like this. The Lord
Chief Justice made it the occasion of one of his common
sense broadsides, using language that transported all identity-
card haters with joy; and in this, at any rate, every one of

the other Judges agreed with him. 'This Court,' he said, 'wishes to express its emphatic approval of the way in which the Magistrates dealt with this case by granting the defendant an absolute discharge. Because the police have powers, it does not follow that they ought to exercise them on all occasions or as a matter of routine' (which was roughly what they were doing about identity cards). 'From what we have been told it is obvious that the police now, as a matter of routine, demand the production of National Registration Cards whenever they stop or interrogate a motorist for whatever cause . . . This Act was passed for security purposes: it was never intended for the purposes for which it is now being used.'

There followed almost at once a letter from the Home Secretary to Chief Constables, reciting Lord Goddard's remarks and resulting in this injunction to the police: 'In future, the police will demand the production of identity cards only when it is absolutely necessary; for example, in cases where there is reason to suspect serious crime, or when the person concerned is suspected of being a deserter or absentee without leave from H.M. Forces.' The fact that this instruction to the police seemed to have general public approval, coupled with the expectation that food rationing would remain for some years and National Insurance for ever, gave identity cards a new but restricted lease of life. They went on being mildly useful without really being much of a nuisance; but whereas no one wept when, a few months later, the National Registration Act was repealed altogether, most of the M.P.s who congratulated the Government on its decision took the opportunity to give the identity card a parting kick, and there were, in fact, a few of the bonfires for which Sir Willam Darling had been longing. There was for a month or two some official pretence that people were remembering their identity numbers just *in case* one of the Ministries might forget who somebody was, but this soon took its place alongside the contemporary fiction

that, just in case, everyone was carefully preserving his
gas-mask.

Two years later Willcock, now nationally famous as 'the
man who got rid of identity cards,' was addressing a Liberal
meeting in London when suddenly, saying 'Mr Chairman,
I don't think I can go on,' he sat down and died. He was
fifty-eight, and apparently in full vigour. Many such men
have changed the course of English law: they have been
prisoners, jurors, judges, writers, contenders in many guises
for the freedoms that have seemed at the time the most
dear because the most in danger. Among them all, we could
remember Clarence Henry Willcock as the patron saint of
anonymity.

III

THE
IDENTIFICATION PARADE

ERHAPS you will tell my Lord and the jury, in your own words, exactly what happened then?'

'A man sprang out of the bushes, and——'

'Do you see that man in Court?'

The next moment can often be a little painful. I have seen witnesses point (a) to the Governor of Brixton Prison, sitting in the Old Bailey dock on one of his routine visits, (b) to a detective sergeant waiting for the clerk of the court to sign the expenses sheet relating to a previous case, (c) to a P.A. reporter, and (d) to the probation officer. Usually, of course, they point at once to the prisoner in the dock; and it is noteworthy that in these cases they often have the grace to look a little embarrassed, like a grown and half-sober man asked by a police doctor to touch the tip of his own nose.

A few years ago it used to be necessary, when a prisoner was indicted as an habitual criminal, for the prosecution to prove by the calling of witnesses that since the age of sixteen he had been three times convicted of serious crime. Three different police officers, often from widely-separated parts of the country, would go into the witness-box.

'Were you present,' prosecuting counsel would ask the first one, 'at Chester Assizes on 4th November, 1931, when Richard Jones was convicted of housebreaking and larceny and sentenced to eighteen months imprisonment?'

'I was, sir.'

'Do you see Richard Jones in court today?'

'I do, sir. There he is.'

The other two police officers would do the same in turn, each, of course, also producing a record of the conviction. It was seldom that one of them gave any theatrical start of surprise; but very occasionally a young and serious-minded constable would glance perfunctorily at one or two other people before letting his eyes light upon the figure in the dock. It showed a nice spirit, long dead in the case-hardened habitués of the Central Criminal Court, but the general atmosphere made it easy to look direct into the dock with a straight face, and the prisoner, anyway, was not disputing what was said about his past. Nowadays the necessary proof of identity is done by the production of fingerprint records. For reasons I try to explain in Chapter V, no one thinks of challenging those.

But even this kind of identification is neither available nor adequate in the earliest stages of a criminal prosecution. Any witness who has run after a suspect in the street will, of course, have to face this kind of thing:

'How far was he in front of you?'

'I should say about thirty yards.'

'All the time?'

'About that, yes.'

'Now, at what point did you lose sight of him?'

'I didn't lose sight of him.'

'No? You say he ran down Queen Street towards the market, and turned to the left into Baker's Court?'

'Yes.'

'Thank you. Can you see round corners?'

'No.'

'Then would you tell the Court how it was that with thirty yards between you, you never lost sight of my client at a right angle corner, with large buildings between you?'

He can't. There are very few cases in which the prosecution can get along without strict proof of some kind that the prisoner is the same man as the one who committed the

offence. The mists of antiquity have closed over the date
when this unavoidable necessity first gave rise to what is
now called the identification parade.

When the police have arrested a man on suspicion that he
is the man who has committed an offence, they can strengthen
the case against him if the prosecutor or other witnesses
can pick him out, unaided in any way, from a sufficient
number of similar-looking people to afford a reasonable
chance that they will choose wrongly and to guard against
lucky guesses.

Accordingly, about half an hour before the time fixed
for the 'parade,' plain clothes policemen go out of the
station to find willing participants from among passers-by
in the street. Some agree—probably the majority—out of
curiosity; others out of fear. Some shake their heads and
walk on; others break into a trot, They vary greatly in
willingness. They are not altogether pleased at the thinly-
clothed implication that they look like crooks. They are often
suspicious, and want to know, when the idea has been
briefly explained to them, what happens if the witness's
choice falls upon them.

'You've got nothing to worry about,' they are then told.
'If he picks you out he's wrong, and there is an end to it.
It can't affect you—only the man in custody.'

This comes within a very short distance of being true,
but the distance is just enough to warrant a little reluctance
on the part of the people accosted—of which, more in a
moment.

The declared purpose of an identification parade is 'to
test fairly and adequately the witnesses' ability to recognise
the accused person.' You can get a sudden insight into the
philosophy of personal identity if you imagine for a moment
that you are the person in custody and that the police are
out looking for people like you to come in and stand in line

with you. No, there are no such people, of course: but the
rules had to be framed as though there were. A number
of 'police and public' incidents, followed in some cases by
spirited question-time exchanges in the House of Commons,
have played their part in framing the rules. (An odd point
is that no one has ever complained about not getting paid
for his services: you may get a shilling or two in some
police districts, but in others, where no one does it twice,
it seems to be regarded—by the police authorities—as one
of the honorary privileges of citizenship.) The rules, which
now have the authority of a Home Office advisory letter
to all Chief Constables, emphasise that the witnesses'
attention must never be directed to the suspected person in
particular instead of indifferently to all the people paraded.

Accordingly, they must be prevented from seeing him
before he is paraded, and ought not to have any assistance
from photographs or descriptions. In practice, they do
sometimes see a photograph: it may well be the fact that
one of the witnesses has picked out the prisoner's photograph from a group of about twenty others that has led to
his arrest. These two forms of identification are not mutually
destructive as evidence, but the first greatly weakens the
second and experienced police officers are loth, as a rule, to
have them in combination. And if the court is told that
a 'parade' identification has been preceded by recognition
from a photograph, it can only be told by the defence, since
the mere existence of the police photograph is evidence that
the prisoner at least strongly resembles someone who has
been in trouble before: a nice dilemma for many a defending
counsel.

The suspect is 'placed' (this is the word used) 'among
persons who are as far as possible of the same age, height,
general appearance and position in life.' It is therefore very
lucky that the common run of suspects are people with no
very confident theories about the rights of citizens in general
and of unconvicted prisoners in particular. If a person

B

refuses to be 'placed' in a line of other people for this purpose, the police (in Great Britain at least) have no power to compel him; and even if they had, the use of force would reduce the 'identification' to a farce. Moreover, if his 'general appearance and position in life' derive from prosperity, social standing, and self-confidence, there is not only far greater difficulty in finding his like among passers-by, but less likelihood that they will want to participate and more chance that the suspect will be dissatisfied with them. (He doesn't have to be satisfied with them but the rules require that he be asked, and it is desirable that he should feel that the people brought in do at least look something like him.)

He has to be allowed to choose his own position in the line, changing it if he likes after each witness has been in, and told that he can have his own solicitor or a friend present at the identification. Then the witnesses are brought in, one by one. They must not be allowed to speak to each other, or even catch sight of each other, after going along the line; they must leave by a separate door and go away; and every unauthorised person must be excluded from the room. Witnesses sometimes want to see the prisoner with his hat on or off, in which case all the participants are asked to wear or take off their hats. If they want to see him walk or hear him speak all the people paraded are asked to walk individually or to speak.

Most senior police officers know these rules rather better than the Lord's Prayer, and go to very great trouble to ensure that they are observed. Zeal, in such cases, sometimes beats discretion by several lengths. In one case where the prisoner suddenly announced, just before the parade, that he usually wore spectacles, spectacles were obtained (from the Lost Property Room) for all the other persons paraded; but as none of the other persons was used to them, and even this example of police conscientiousness didn't run to optical tests for all, they all acquired, when they put them on, a myopic look from which the suspect alone was immune. It was a simpler and more effectual resourcefulness, in the case of a suspect with a club foot, that led the police officer in charge to cover all the participants' feet and ankles with rugs.

'Criticism has from time to time been made,' said the Report of the 1929 Royal Commission on Police Powers and Procedure, 'in court and elsewhere, as to the manner in which these identifications are carried out, and attempts have been made to impugn the reliability of the evidence of identity obtained.'

This was a stately acknowledgment of the uproar that followed the case of Major R. O. Sheppard in 1925. The story of the misfortune that befell this distinguished officer of the Army Ordnance Corps invites comparison with the more famous case of Adolf Beck (see Chapter VI). Late in the evening of June 27, 1925, Major Sheppard was walking along Down Street, Piccadilly, when a girl came up to him and said 'I've got you now!' She grabbed his arm and swung him round. He demanded an explanation, and said he would give her in charge. 'You stole my bag and £18,' she cried; 'they know all about you at Hunter Street Police Station.' He was the one, she said, who was going to be given in charge.

He had never seen her before in his life; but since they both seemed intent on 'giving each other in charge,' it was not so eccentric as it sounds that they got into a taxi-cab and drove together to Vine Street Police Station in order to do it. As soon as they got there the girl, whose name was Deltah Dennistoun and who admitted that she was a prostitute, said to the Station Officer: 'This man is wanted by the police at Hunter Street for stealing £18 of mine and a case. They know all about it at Hunter Street.'

'She has made a mistake,' said Major Sheppard. 'I am not the man. I have never seen her before. She accosted me in the street at Piccadilly and accused me of this theft. I denied it and we came here.' But the girl persisted in her accusation, and the police at Vine Street embarked on a course of procedure which, although a lot of it conformed with their practice and regulations at the time, would seem to many present-day policemen to suggest a carefully-cultivated bloody-mindedness. The girl's address, 21, Tavistock Place, happened to be within the area looked after by Hunter Street Police Station, and it was at that time an unchallengeable precept of police procedure that every police station booked its own charges and locked up its own prisoners, turning all others away in the manner immortal-ised by Fred Karno. A Hunter Street offender must be charged at Hunter Street, though he was already at Vine Street, in the custody of the same police force and in the jurisdiction of the same magistrates. Vine Street could only regard him as a short-term guest, though it could (and did) make the term twice as long as it need be by sending to Hunter Street for an escort to collect him, instead of taking him there at once. (And this, by the way, many police officers would still do.) But in Major Sheppard's case, Vine Street filled in a little of the time by arranging an identification parade.

The man who had robbed Miss Dennistoun had told her his address was 58 Jermyn Street, and she had since ascer-tained there that the hall-porter would be prepared to identify him. So the Vine Street police sent round to Jermyn Street for the hall-porter's assistance; and after some hesita-tion he picked out Major Sheppard as a man who stayed at No 58 and whom he knew as Major Trevor. The fact that 'Major Trevor,' a known criminal, was actually arrested some days later, made it possible for Major Sheppard's name to be completely cleared. But the case had aroused such public indignation that the Home Secretary, Sir William Joynson-Hicks, set up a Court of Enquiry under Mr J. F. P. Rawlinson, K.C., M.P., to report upon the

conduct of the police throughout. And the evidence Mr
Rawlinson received makes it possible for us to have a look
at an identification parade from a number of different view-
points. Allowing for a little subjective colour, the accounts
vary in a way that should help anyone trying to assess the
value of eye-witnesses anywhere.

It is important to remember that the 'parade' was held at
about one o'clock in the morning, when the kind of people
to be found in the streets offers a limited choice. However,
at the Rawlinson enquiry later, Sir Patrick Hastings said
that at the time Major Sheppard was dressed in a lounge
suit—'the ordinary suit of clothes a man in his position
would wear. When he was told by the police inspector that
he would be "put up for identification",' went on Sir Patrick,
'a nondescript collection of people were there, probably
brought out of the street. They certainly didn't appear to
be official in any sense of the word.' (No one has ever discovered what Sir Patrick meant by this: was it a complaint
that they were not policemen? But Sir Percival Clarke had
already complained at the Magistrates' Court, on Major
Sheppard's behalf, that 'none of them could be taken for
gentlemen.') Major Sheppard himself told the Court of
Enquiry that 'none of the others looked in the least like
an army officer, and four of them were wearing chokers.'
Later Sir Patrick said that these four were 'without collars
and had handkerchiefs round their necks.' But Police
Sergeant Beard, of Vine Street, swore that they all wore
collars and that three of them were staying at the Piccadilly
Hotel. Two of these, added Detective Sergeant Woods of
Hunter Street, were in dress clothes.

These were not the only conflicts that Mr J. F. P.
Rawlinson had to resolve in making his report to the Home
Secretary. A police inspector said that Major Sheppard was
asked if he was satisfied with the people selected to go on
the parade with him, and said that he was. Major Sheppard

told Mr Rawlinson: 'If I had been given the opportunity I should have objected to all the men who were brought in to be placed with me for identification.' The police witnesses all said that the hall-porter from 58 Jermyn Street picked out Major Sheppard without any hesitation or encouragement. Sir Patrick Hastings described the whole affair like this:

'They stood in line, and Major Sheppard was told to take his place in the line, where he was the object of the most ingenuous interest on the part of everybody. It was a farcical enquiry. He stood in the middle of the line, and everybody at once proceeded to examine him with the greatest interest. The men on both sides of him were looking towards him, and the police were looking on to see what happened. The hall-porter, who went along the line, said that he wasn't sure who was the man; but urged on by the hypnotic influence of the police and the men who were looking at Major Sheppard, the hall-porter at length walked up and touched him.'

A strange feature of the Major Sheppard case was that, although the police discovered *before* he was committed for trial at the Old Bailey that a mistake had been made, and told the magistrate that the charge against him was un-founded, the committal for trial was nevertheless proceeded with. It may possibly have been thought that the unfortunate Major's feelings would be better mollified by a jury's verdict of 'not guilty' than a magistrate's assurance that the whole thing was a mistake; but the costs in the case were enor-mously increased by this needless step. And as it turned out, the case never earned a 'not guilty' verdict. It happened in the days of Grand Juries, when every case was 'vetted' before the petty juries got down to the business of trial, and the Grand Jury could 'throw out the Bill' in any case where the prosecution, on its own evidence alone, seemed to them inadequate or misconceived. The Bill in Major Sheppard's case was thrown out because the Recorder, Sir Ernest Wild, K.C. made it plain that the Major had no case to answer. 'The proof of identification,' said the Recorder, 'rests entirely on the evidence of this woman. I need not remind you of the perils of mistaken identity, or of the terrible miscarriages of justice that have happened through witnesses making perfectly honest mistakes in identifying a person.'

Later, in open court, the recognisances in the case were discharged, at the instance of Mr Eustace Fulton for the Director of Public Prosecutions. Mr Fulton said that the one man who had prevented the case from developing into a grave miscarriage of justice was Detective Sergeant Woods of Hunter Street. 'He was not satisfied that the evidence of identity was correct. He went on with his investigations, and on July 10' (that is, a fortnight after Major Sheppard's night at Vine Street) 'he arrested on other charges a man who bore a striking resemblance to Major Sheppard. The new man was put up with twelve other men, and Miss Dennistoun immediately picked him out.' (She may have been one of those unhesitating pickers-out who can be as big an embarrassment to the police as the zanies who systematically confess to every murder.) 'In those circumstances the Director of Public Prosecutions thought it right that immediate steps should be taken to clear Major Sheppard of the charge made against him.'

But Sir Percival Clarke, who was there to defend Major Sheppard, found this rather less than satisfactory. There were serious grounds for complaint against the police, quite apart from the farcical nature of the 'identification' at Vine Street Police Station. 'My client at once asked for an inspector to be called,' said Sir Percival. 'He showed him proofs of his identity and rank; he said that he was in charge of the Gunpowder Magazine in Hyde Park and that he was perfectly well known by the police at Hyde Park Police Station. The officer in charge, referring to my client's identity papers, said 'How do we know that they are not stolen, too?' (This was emphatically denied.) 'The police refused to communicate with the Provost Marshal, or the Major's

Commanding officer, or the police at Hyde Park.' And so forth.

The Sheppard case involved several other criticisms of police procedure. Some of them were met by changes in the law: the Criminal Justice Act of 1925 empowered the police, though it still seems hardly credible that they needed statutory sanction for it, to release on bail an arrested person about whom their enquiries could not soon be completed and who, therefore, had not yet been formally charged with an offence. (This would have made it possible to let Major Sheppard, released on bail from Vine Street, go himself to Hunter Street the next day, instead of locking him up to await a Hunter Street escort.) The Home Office clarified the existing instructions to the police about the conduct of identification parades. The 1929 Royal Commission on Police Powers and Procedure drew on Mr J. F. P. Rawlinson's report to the Home Secretary for several of its recommendations. And generally it may be said, perhaps, that Major Sheppard did not suffer in vain.

But since the Royal Commission on Police Powers reported, there have been a number of cases in which the reliability of identification parades has been 'impugned' to some purpose. The case of Adolf Beck (see Chapter VI) had gone considerably further than impugnation, but in 1953 a case at West London Magistrates' Court showed once more that these parades can have the most deplorable consequences and led the Metropolitan Magistrate to remark: 'This case underlines the terrible dangers of identity parades; it is not surprising that juries and magistrates are very chary of convicting on them.' The story was as follows:

A lorry driver from Colne, in Lancashire, hitch-hiked to London on 25th January, 1953, to surrender to police bail on a charge of stealing ten tons of flour by means of a trick. He was said to have called one day with his lorry at a Chelsea flour-mill, and declared that he had come from a well-known firm that made doughnuts to collect ten tons of flour. A woman clerk believed what he said, the flour was loaded on to his lorry, and off he went. The invoice for the flour was duly sent by post to the doughnut firm, and on receipt of it they denied having either received or ordered any flour. The lorry driver's description having been given to the police, he was arrested in London and 'put up for identification' at a parade.

Two witnesses picked him out as the thief.

He was accordingly charged with the larceny of ten tons of flour, and after formal evidence, which he strongly denied, he was remanded—on bail once more. But before the business of the West London Court was over for that day, the Chelsea flour mill telephoned to say that their ten tons of flour had been traced to the premises of a firm in Newport. The doughnut firm, it turned out, employed transport contractors, who in turn employed sub-contractors. And it was a sub-contractor's lorry driver, not the man charged, who in pursuance of a quite legitimate transaction had driven away a ten-ton load of flour and taken it to Newport. Accordingly the police offered no evidence and the lorry driver was discharged. The episode shows, as many similar ones have done, that although there may not be very much danger to the eight or more innocent members of an identification parade, there is indeed a terrible danger to an innocent suspect.

In 1927 the Court of Criminal Appeal had to quash the conviction of a man named Charles Hardcastle Lee, because a witness who had picked him out at a police station parade was unable to identify him in court; and then by way of making matters worse (in an effort to make them better) the prisoner was trapped into admitting that the witness had picked him out at the parade. 'This prisoner admitted,' said Lord Hewart, the Lord Chief Justice, 'that he had been identified by someone not on oath who, when put on oath, was unable to maintain the previous identification. The conviction cannot stand.' The oath, indeed, often comes into its own in questions of identification. Later in the same year a man said at North London Magistrates' Court: 'Well, I wouldn't swear they were the men.' The magistrate knew what oaths and swearing meant to some people. 'But would you bet on it?' he asked the witness. 'I certainly would!' was the emphatic answer. The essence of the sporting instinct is to be ready to act on something less than 'the whole truth.'

Witnesses brought in front of an identification parade know from the beginning that somewhere, among the 'eight or more,' there stands the man whom the police suspect. Under such circumstances a passing likeness can become a positive identity. Some witnesses, remarked the 1929 Royal Commission, 'owing to a faulty memory or lack of powers of observation, are far less successful and may tend unconsciously to identify the person who most resembles their recollection of the culprit, disregarding, apparently, the alternative that he may not be present at all. It is significant, however, that none of the critics of the existing system have suggested any alternative method which would be more fair to persons put up for identification.'

But they had. A number of critics suggested that there should always be at least two parades, one of them 'blank;' in one of them, that is to say, the person suspected would not be present. Each witness would be told that he was going to see two separate parades and that the suspect would be in only one of them. They could be held simultaneously in separate rooms, each witness going straight on from the first to the second (unless he picked on somebody in the first). The Royal Commission did not entirely overlook this idea, but they thought there were 'certain obvious objections, particularly the difficulties already experienced in persuading suitable persons to attend a parade.' This, in fact, seems the only objection that can be called 'obvious,' and there need be no doubt about its authorship. Throughout the voluminous Minutes of Evidence on which the 1929 Report is based, all the criticism of identification parades as at present conducted came from lawyers and reformers, and it was often vehement; while all the praise came from the police, and it was always lukewarm.

There was much complaint, after Major Sheppard's case, that the people in the parade were often allowed to know which one of them was the suspect: hence the 'craning of necks' as they stood in line, or, to borrow the language of the 1929 Report, the risk for the prisoner that 'the attitude of the other persons forming the parade may unconsciously assist the witnesses to identify him.' But 'the present instruction which allows the accused, if he so desires, to change his position after each witness has left, though intended to prevent unfairness to him, makes it impossible to conceal his identity from the other paraders. It was therefore suggested that all the paraders should change their positions after each witness had left, or that they should all walk about while the witnesses looked at them. The first of these devices is now fairly commonly used; but the second, though it might sometimes produce the theoretically ideal parade, would often mean in practice that the police had to find eight men who were excessively knock-kneed or bandy, club-footed, cork-legged, or temporarily wearing shoes too small. You can see all this in the frigidity of the police evidence before the Royal Commission.

In Great Britain, no one has yet forced the issue about submitting to compulsory processes of identification. Our criminals are a fairly docile lot. What right have the British police to require a suspect, even though he may have been charged already with one offence, to toe the line with a number of other persons in order that his appearance may be studied and compared? No one bothers whether they have the right or not: no one challenges it in the courts. It is difficult to find any authority for it, certainly in England. The Scottish courts have decided that the Scottish police have power to take the finger prints of a suspect by force, if need be, and they occasionally do it. In England, the power to do this is carefully withheld from the police, who must as a rule await the prisoner's removal to a remand prison, where the Prison Rules authorise it provided the consent of a Justice of the Peace has been obtained. (See Chapter V). But nowhere has it been necessary to hold that the police have a right to 'put you up' for identification. Our prisoners take it all as part of what is coming to them. Is is that they genuinely desire to co-operate with the police, once the hand has fallen on their shoulder? This is not the case in the U.S.A.

In the United States the procedure has often been challenged. In Georgia in 1940 it was held proper to 'compel an accused person to submit to a police line-up, whereby he is placed alongside other persons or prisoners to be viewed by witnesses to one or more criminal offences' (*Meriwether v. State,* Ga. App. 667). This means that someone had been prepared to spend money and time fighting that proposition in the courts. In Texas in 1942 the courts even found it necessary to hold that a police officer could lawfully compel a prisoner to walk about in a room, so that he could be watched by identifying witnesses. (*Fundesburgh v. State,* 144 Tex. G.R.35). And the Texas case went so far as to say that it made no difference that the arrest and detention of the suspect actually turned out to be unlawful anyway.

The American Courts have also been put to the necessity of holding that the police may lawfully require a prisoner to change his clothing—to put on a coat or take off a jacket. Justice Holmes had this to say in 1910 in *Holt v. United States* (218 U.S.245): 'The prohibition of compelling a man in a criminal case to be a witness against himself is a prohibition of the use of physical or moral compulsion to extort communications from him, not an exclusion of his body as evidence, when it may be material. The objection in principle would forbid a jury to look at a prisoner and compare his features with a photograph.' The Texas police have also won the right to make a man take off his spectacles so that witnesses can see his features better (*Rutherford v. State,* 1938), and the police of New York can show you chapter and verse for the proposition that they can lawfully make a man have a long overdue shave and haircut, when he has grown long hair and whiskers by refusing the services of a remand prison barber (*People v. Strauss,* 1940).

The countries of the British Commonwealth follow, in the main, all the devices of police procedure that have acquired in England a kind of Common Law dignity by not being challenged. But the identification parade has had an uphill fight, of which one important case—from Melbourne—may be considered as typical. It is to be found in the law books as *Craig v. The King* (49 Commonwealth L.R. 429).

On 31st January, 1936, a clerk employed by the Comptroller of Stamps for Victoria was taking £1,760 in a bag to a Melbourne Bank. He was just getting into a taxicab with a fellow-employee, when two men with automatic pistols held up the cab, shot the fellow-employee dead, seized the bag and dashed off in a waiting car, driven by a third man. The car eventually (and presumably by mistake) went into the yard of a municipal building used for burning refuse; and there one of the bandits got out and ran back through the yard entrance, while the other two ran across the yard, spoke to the yard superintendent for a moment, and then went out by a second gate. A pistol found at the place where the shot was fired was proved by a ballistics expert to be the one used to fire it.

Nine months later three men were arrested for the robbery and murder, and the business of getting them identified began. Each of the three men was 'submitted for scrutiny' by a long succession of witnesses. Criminal procedure in Victoria, at least at that time, regarded it as evidence of identification when a witness pointed to a prisoner in the dock and said 'That's the man;' but in this case another method was relied upon which may be thought even less convincing. Each man was 'submitted for scrutiny,' standing alone in a bright light in what was called a 'view room' at the police station. And even so, two of the witnesses at this latter ceremony were first shown photographs of the men they were to see.

The three men were tried before Sir Frederick Mann, Chief Justice of Victoria, and a jury. In Victoria a jury is allowed a maximum of six hours to reach a verdict; and after a six-hour retirement this one had to be sent for. It had failed to agree in respect of two of the prisoners, but found the third not guilty on the direction of the Chief Justice. The other two were retried three months later, and sentenced to death.

They sought leave to appeal to the Full Court of the Supreme Court of Victoria, one of their grounds of appeal being that there had been no 'identification parade;' and their application was dismissed because, said the Full Court, there was no rule of law or practice to require the police to employ the 'parade' method of identification, or to require the trial judge to warn the jury that other methods of 'identification' were of inferior value as evidence. Then the two men applied for leave to appeal to the High Court of Australia, and this was considered in June 1937, eighteen months after the murder. Here are the points put forward for the appellants by their counsel, who quoted, among many other precedents, the case of Adolf Beck (see Chapter VI).

(1) Evidence of identity based on personal impressions and given by witnesses not previously acquainted

with the prisoners, if not supported by other evidence, is as a general rule unsafe.

(2) It has no value unless it is proved to be based on the witnesses' unaided recollection of the physical appearance or characteristics of a prisoner looked at under incriminating circumstances.

(3) It has no value if it is shown to be based on 'recognition' in the dock or in a police view-room, or any other circumstances, such as the showing of official photographs to the witness, which suggest to the witness that the prisoner is in fact the offender or even a suspect.

The High Court unanimously granted the two men leave to appeal, then allowed the appeal, and then ordered (under the Victorian Crimes Act, 1928, which authorised such a procedure) that they be tried all over again. Back in Victoria, they came this time before Mr Justice Macfarlan—and again the jury disagreed. At a fourth trial the Crown, at long last, entered a *nolle prosequi* and the men were discharged. The interest of all this crystallises in the following remarks of the Judges in the High Court of Australia:

'The learned Judge who tried the prisoners left the matter to the jury without any definite warning of the dangers which such a method of identification' (i.e. the 'view-room' and the dock) 'is in other jurisdictions considered to involve. Among other things he said: "There has been a most acrimonious debate about what is the best way for persons to be identified by the police, and it is neither your business nor mine to say which is the best way . . . It is said a more proper way would be to put him amongst others of about his own size and kind, and let him be picked out. If you take the view, as probably you will, that to pick out a man in the dock, or under the lights by himself, does not add anything to the identification, then the identification loses something it might have if he picked out the accused from a number of others. If a man is pointed out to a witness by himself under a light, or still more in the dock, that in effect is an effort by the police to force him into saying 'That is the man'; it is the use of suggestion—'of course he must be the man, I see him in the dock accused of murder and he must be the man' " '

But this was not going far enough for the High Court Judges. 'As the responsibility of convicting must rest with the jury,' the High Court judgement went on, 'their appreciation of the question is an important consideration; and in a case where the method of identification is open to the objections we have discussed, they should be clearly warned of the dangers which, according to the accepted view, do exist. In the present case we think the observations of the learned Judge do not amount to a fulfilment of this requirement. Following the view apparently prevailing in the Supreme Court of Victoria, he treated the matter as one depending upon advice between rival systems, between different schools of thought.'

And two of the Australian High Court Justices, Evatt and McTiernan, added a joint opinion in these pithy terms:

'An honest witness who says "The prisoner is the man who drove the car," while appearing to affirm a simple, clear, and impressive proposition, is really asserting

(1) that he observed the driver,
(2) that the observation became impressed on his mind,
(3) that he still retains the original impression,
(4) that such impression has not been affected, altered, or replaced by published portraits of the prisoner, and,
(5) that the resemblance between the original impression and the prisoner is sufficient to base a judgement, not of resemblance but of identity.'

That is identification. By that standard, a police identi-

fication parade, though always cast in a tragic mould for
the prisoner, often slips over into farce for everyone else.

These parades are held more often at police stations than
anywhere else. But they quite often take place at Magistrates'
Courts, when additional charges are being brought against
a prisoner and fresh victims of his crimes have been got to
the court to see whether he is 'the man'; and they sometimes
enliven the monotony of prison.

At a court, the participants are sought in the street, in the
usual way. At a prison, they are prisoners. This is not to
say that they are volunteers on the 'you-you-and-you'
principle: they are asked if they would care to assist at an
identification parade, and the only ones who unhesitatingly
decline are those who fear, not entirely without reason, that
some further crime may by that means be actually (and even
justifiably) pinned upon themselves. The others welcome
anything as a break in prison routine. Their own 'civvy'
clothes are got out and brushed for the occasion, or they
are fitted out from stores; and the man put up for identification among them takes his chance whether the prison, at
that moment, can offer a selection of eight men who are
similar in 'age, height, general appearance, and position in
life.' It says something for conditions in a modern prison that
its inhabitants can be thought eligible, even though the
official standard of verisimilitude be not exacting, to dare
comparison with the unconvicted.

I find it possible to end this chapter only by resisting
a temptation to which I have always been prone: namely
to discuss *per se* the people who are invited into police
stations and other places to take part in these frequently
deadly charades. Who are they? Why does one never meet
them afterwards? I know that one never meets the people
who say 'Don't know' in the Gallup Polls, but this may be
because they don't know that a Gallup Poll has hit them.

To get into an identification parade involves a sort of appointment, almost an election: you are told what is required of you, and if your responses are too daft you are dismissed with a nod. But after the parade is over and the members have been thanked and sent away, with or without their eighteenpence, what happens to them? All through the long disputes about what happened in the Major Sheppard case, no member of that parade came forward to say that he was there and could relate exactly what had happened. They are as anonymous, *ex post facto*, as jurors: more so, because a juror's name and address are known to the court officials, and if in some super palace of justice he carved his initials on the polished maple of a brand-new jury-box they could write to him.

Police witnesses before the 1929 Royal Commission on Police Powers and Procedure were asked whether they took the names and addresses of these people. Always, said a few. Never, said the great majority, adding that such people were never wanted again and that their lulled suspicions about the back-lash of an identification parade would be fanned into fierce flame by such a request. One thing will be obvious to anyone who has tried to get the names of independent witnesses to one of the more generous acts of indecent exposure: anyone who has any fear that the policemanly 'Name and address, sir?' is likely to result some day in a subpoena will be nameless, without occupation, and of no fixed abode. The bright burden of identity, at these parades, is lifted from the innocent participants to hover about the suspect, leaving the rest featureless and unknown and without interest.

IV

VERBAL PERSONALITY

ONE of the strangest quirks of human personality is related to the power of ideas, and of the words by which they are identified and communicated, to change the personality and, in time, to change almost the essential identity of men and women. The law provides some entertaining instances of this.

Begin with the policeman. A police recruit is hardly more than a boy; and it seems to be part of the system in this as in most countries that he shall come from a social *milieu* in which, naturally enough, no thought is given to training for authority and leadership. It may be protested that our police system is not founded on these qualities, that we have neither the need nor the taste for minor uniformed führer-figures ordering our lives by the enforcement of regulations; we like our policeman to be one of us, a man we know and like and can comfortably co-operate with. Much effort, ink, and oratory is spent in fostering the wistful illusion that this is what we have got. But the truth is that in many of the emergencies that the policeman faces in the course of his duty, he must take charge of a situation in a way that requires the obedience of others. Neither as a boy at school nor as a police recruit in training has he ever been prepared for it.

The consequence is that the putting on of a police uniform does something almost catastrophic to the personality of some young men. Lacking the rare qualities of leadership and authority, they find that they must either acquire counterfeit copies or go in for bluster. Bluster seems to work fairly well, in this country. We are a docile race, with a puritan sense of unexpiated sin and a facility for skin-deep propitiation. To see one of our solid citizens explaining something across the desk of a police station is often an agonising exhibition of maimed personality; and a police-man gets accustomed to a special language of ingratiation from the motorist who differs consciously from himself in education and outlook, though the same policeman is happy enough that the lorry driver should call him 'mate.' The process does much to produce a state of mind in which a policeman becomes totally identified with the laws which he has to enforce, so that a dog without a collar, a child smoking, an expired car licence, or a stationary barrow-boy become personal affronts. I have indeed seen a policeman (though this is rare) beside himself with indignation over an emptied dustbin standing on the pavement at 10.15 a.m., where 10 a.m. is the latest time for the removal of emptied dustbins into the premises where they belong.

The acquisition of a kind of legal personality is a logical extension of this; and it is aided by the inescapable need for a special language. The function of police language, which produces a verbal personality as distinct as the parson's or the psycho-analyst's, is twofold: it must provide, as a means of expression in countless police reports, a common ground for the romantic writer and the semi-literate, with a powerful discipline to control the pens of both, and it must supply a protective armour against the casuistry of lawyers. It moulds the policeman, who may have begun his police life as a plumbing or engineering or shop-keeping or soldiering identity, into a legal identity.

Perhaps there has been too much fun about this. It has often been poked, moreover, by those who are for the same reasons richly comic: lawyers still find it possible, after a century and a half of listening to police evidence, to be amused or annoyed at the little pomposities of the jargon.

'That means he was going East, does it?' they ask, when a police witness says that a motorist was 'proceeding in an Easterly direction.' The policeman often agrees that it does, because the court is laughing at him and he is not equipped for semantic argument. But his own phrase is an inherited one. It makes careful allowance for the fact that the usual verbs of movement—'going,' 'coming,' and others—are inexact and relative, often wrongly suggesting the observer's position, viewpoint, and mental attitude. The phrase also means that he did not use a compass to confirm the direction of movement; he can say no more than that the direction was Easterly, or roughly East.

And yet if there is such a thing as an absolute creature of verbal process, it is the lawyer. Study him from the jury-box, and pick out the peaks of identity as they go majestically by:

'It matters not, members of the jury . . .'

'It is my respectful submission that . . .'

'A person of unimpeachable character . . .'

'Subject to what my Lord, in his greater wisdom, may say to you . . .'

'. . . to suggest therefore to your Lordship, with the utmost respect, that your Lordship may find it possible, in dealing with this man, to take a certain course . . .'

And so forth. They, and only they, say 'oh-casion' for occasion, and will never speak of nearness when there are phrases like 'close proximity.' After ten years' practice they talk like it everywhere except on the golf course. They are legal identities, fair game for the dramatist and rather amusing to all but the litigant.

One of the most remarkable instances of synthesised identity, owing much to the way in which personality can be built, or warped, by a too-close acquaintance with the law, was the case of Horatio Bottomley. This almost legendary swindler and demagogue used to claim that Bradlaugh was his father—though he did not begin this particular imposture until some years after the death of the Bethnal Green tailor's foreman to whom that distinction really belonged. His mother was a niece of George Jacob Holyoake, a man who devoted a turbulent life to the cause of the working classes and the co-operative movement. Bottomley, in turn, devoted the latter part of his life to the seduction and betrayal of the same people, by the promotion of gigantic and fraudulent lotteries designed to exploit music-hall patriotism on a scale that could have won the approval of Adolf Hitler himself. It may have been Bottomley's initial misfortune that his second job (at the age of about fourteen and a half) was as office-boy to a firm of solicitors in Coleman Street. In the 1920s there was a song about him in the H.M.S. Pinafore rhythm:

> When I was a lad I served a turn
> As office-boy in an attorney's firm.
> I cleaned the windows and I scrubbed the floor,
> And I polished up the knocker on the big front door.
> And as I did the polishing it seemed to me
> You could swindle quite a lot without an LL.B.

He got no LL.B., but neither did he scrub any floors. He served writs, swore affidavits, assimilated jargon, and learned the infinite patience with which an experienced lawyer is able to endure the misfortunes of his clients. And five years later, when he had learned to write shorthand, he got himself a job as a reporter with George Walpole & Co., who were (and still are) the official reporters to the High Court. Thus in the Old Bailey, the Court of Criminal Appeal and elsewhere, Bottomley studied the routine and deportment which in later years he so delighted to ape—and to lampoon; and there never was an apter student of manner without substance, of a particular elocution without the tradition that gave it birth. From that time there began the assumption by this man of an identity in which he came to believe absolutely (although, in the bath or somewhere, he may have had introspective moments of doubt). It sustained him not only on public platforms, where he could earn £500 in a night as a stentorian lecturer and from which, in the Kaiser's war, he so passionately exhorted youth to go out and die for the country he was plundering: it kept him going under the strain of company promotions and public bond swindles that brought him in about £5,000,000, and sustained him through 260 separate bankruptcy petitions.

Those who have encountered the typical litigant-in-person will probably agree that such people conform to a type, an outstanding characteristic of which is an assumption that the external world is composed entirely of listeners. They may begin life normally enough, as little Bottomley did in the Birmingham orphanage school to which G. J. Holyoake sent him on becoming his guardian in 1863. But prolonged pursuit of litigation results in a change of identity which is complete and irreversible, the assumption of an aggressive role that holds the rest of society at bay instead of merging more or less comfortably with it.

We may not agree with Edmund Burke's rather smug distribution of the more sterling qualities among those 'happily born', but we can leave him with the last word about what may be called the law's natural children: 'The law is in my opinion,' he said, 'one of the first and noblest of human sciences; a science which does more to quicken and invigorate the understanding than all the other kinds of learning put together; but it is not apt, except in persons very happily born, to open and to liberalise the mind in exactly the same proportion.'

V

FINGER PRINTS

On the widely-spaced occasions when Charles Peace got caught in the act of burglary or housebreaking, he was taken to be a first offender and treated as such. He can't have looked like one, but a man is not to be punished for his looks. And until 1882 even in France, where the science of 'judicial identity' was born, there would have been no means—except the rarest of accidents —of knowing that Peace was a man with a long criminal record.

The story of Alphonse Bertillon's pioneer work in the technique of identification has been told in dozens of authoritative books, and we need spend little time on that or the finger print system that has virtually supplanted it. As a junior clerk in the Prefecture of Police in Paris, Bertillon rescued himself from the monotony of filling up useless 'forms of identity' (which seldom really identified any one criminal with his photograph) by working out a series of living descriptions of the human face and appearance that made the uniqueness of every individual capable of absolute proof. He called it the *portrait parlé*: other people called it anthropometry; but he had to die before it came to be called the Bertillon System and by that time, even in France, it had become a mere adjunct to the finger print method: in England it was used only from 1894 until 1900. Bertillon greeted the new science of finger prints with extreme scepticism, and indeed it was not until after his death that even the leading experts in that field actually came to understand that no two single finger print

56

patterns are ever alike. Till then, it was largely a science
of disproof, in that it could usually show conclusively
that a suspected person did *not* commit the crime. Its
status as a source of positive testimony came into its own
later.

But Bertillon had an interesting connection with the
greatest case of mistaken identity in the whole history of
crime—*l'affaire Dreyfus*. Captain Dreyfus, of the French
Ministry of War, was arrested on a charge of treason in
1894, and is generally considered to have owed this misfortune (for he was entirely innocent) to the fact that he was
a Jew: the French Army at that time was violently anti-
semitic. A man named Gobert, of the Bank of France, had
told the police that a torn-up document delivered at the
'Deuxième Bureau' by a former member of the German
Military Attache's staff was in a handwriting very similar
to Captain Dreyfus's. It contained vital military secrets.
Bertillon's growing reputation as an expert in anthropometic
identification problems seems to have suggested to the
Ministry of War that he must know about handwriting too.
There never was the smallest foundation for this, but
Bertillon obviously shared the Ministry's opinion that there
was. Flattered by the invitation, he got to work with graph-
paper and callipers, and reported fairly promptly that the
letter was written by Dreyfus. He stuck to this opinion even
when, five years later, Captain Esterhazy confessed to the
crime and Dreyfus, brought back from his imprisonment on
Devil's Island, was pardoned. This happened because at that
time a Colonel Picquart was in charge of the Deuxième
Bureau, and fresh reasons came under his notice for exactly
similar suspicions to those which had led to Dreyfus's
conviction—but this time involving a Captain Esterhazy.
He got a specimen of Esterhazy's writing, compared it
with the suspect document, and then showed both to
Bertillon.

Bertillon's verdict was unhesitating and emphatic. 'Any fool,' he said, 'should be able to see without difficulty that both these documents were written by Dreyfus.'

'You are mistaken, M. Bertillon,' said Colonel Picquart. 'they were both written, quite recently, by another officer altogether.'

Bertillon was furious. The Jews, he stormed, had made the documents in exact imitation of Dreyfus's handwriting. There is no record of what he thought this extraordinary behaviour on the part of 'the Jews' would have proved, or why he thought they should busy themselves in pouring further hot water upon an innocent Jew who had already been five years on Devil's Island. But this episode brought a smile to the faces of the sceptics about 'handwriting experts' that has never quite gone away. To this day, indeed, there are people with much experience of the criminal courts who wonder how any handwriting expert can keep a straight face when he sees another one; and their wonder has been increased by cases as recent as that of John Halliday Christie, the multiple murderer of Rillington Place.

Bertillon was cured of his scepticism about finger prints, however, by a murder case that he investigated at an apartment in the Faubourg Saint Honoré in 1902. He photographed some blood stains on the glass door of a china cabinet, from which some articles had been stolen—presumably by the murderer. They were in fact the imprints of fingers that had blood on them, and when he compared them with the fingerprints of a man who was suspected of the crime there were sufficient points of similarity to identify the suspect without doubt as the murderer, and he was convicted.

By that time, finger prints had been in use for over forty years. That famous Indian civil servant, Sir William

Herschel, had used them since 1858 as a kind of signature for native employees who were unable to write; a Scottish medical missionary, Henry Faulds, had been urging their suitability for identifying the absent criminal who had left his prints at the scene of his crime; and Sir Francis Galton, the illustrious founder of the science of eugenics, urged upon the Home Office in 1894 that they were of obvious value for purposes of criminal identification. Four years later an Inspector-General of Police in Bengal, Mr Edward Henry, (he became Commissioner of the London Metropolitan Police in 1903) worked out the system of grouping and classifying finger prints without which, of course, it could have had little more value than a collection of studio portraits. Galton wrote in 1892 that the chances against two finger prints coinciding were sixty-four thousand millions to one, but most of the finger print enthusiasts have since agreed on the addition of several noughts to the larger figure; and after a gestation period prolonged for upwards of forty years by the most undignified scramble for kudos that has ever disgraced the path of science, a finger print bureau is now to be found in every capital city in the world. The Bureau at New Scotland Yard has the finger prints (each with an unflattering biography) of more than 1,500,000 offenders.

In the great criminal man-hunt, of course, the finger print experts are all on the side of the hounds. Expert evidence *against* finger prints either does not exist or is not available in the defence of the kind of prisoner who usually has finger print evidence to contend with. So the expert witness from the Finger Print Bureau cannot be seriously tested, and what he says in the witness-box is absolutely stereotyped. Doctors, psychiatrists, firearms experts, archi-tects, accountants, dozens of specialists of many kinds have to face cross-examination by conscientious lawyers who have been mugging up the subject for the occasion. But every court comes to regard finger print evidence as infallible, because no one can find any way to shake it.

No one? In 1938 a man stood before the Croydon Borough Sessions on a housebreaking charge. He was defending himself. At the close of the case for the prosecution, the Chairman asked him what he proposed to do.

'You can address the jury from where you are now, in the dock,' he said, 'in which case you will not be on oath, and no one can ask you questions about what you have said. Or you can go into the witness-box and tell your story upon oath, in which case you will probably be cross-examined. I might even ask you one or two things myself. Which do you want to do?'

'I don't need to move from here,' said the prisoner confidently, 'so long as the jury can see what I'm doing. I want a piece of plastic rubber and a mirror, please.'

Unorthodox as this appetite must have seemed, the plastic rubber and the mirror were procured—perhaps from his personal property down in the cells. Everybody watched him closely, including those who were pretending not to.

'Now, members of the jury,' he said, 'the police witnesses have told you that they found my finger print on a bottle. I'm going to tell you that they put that finger print on there themselves, *after* they'd got me in custody and taken my finger prints on a paper form. It's the only way they could get me. It's the only bit of evidence against me. Well, it's faked evidence; and I'm going to show you just how it's done. You watch this very closely, ladies and gentlemen.'

And he proceeded to take an impression of a complaisant prison officer's finger by means of the plastic rubber, and from that he made an impression direct on to the piece of mirror.

'There you are, ladies and gentlemen,' he said, and he passed the mirror to an usher, who handed it to the interested jury. It bore an unmistakable finger print.

The Chairman had a look at it. 'Yes,' he said. 'I think the Scotland Yard finger print officer had better be recalled.'

The Scotland Yard man came back into the witness-box. The mirror was handed to him. 'What do you think about that?' asked the Chairman.

'This impression, my Lord,' said the finger print expert, 'will be a reversed impression. The ridges on the prison officer's fingers appear here as furrows, and the furrows as ridges.'

'Oh, that's all right,' said the prisoner, unabashed. He produced from among his belongings a plaster-cast finger print of someone else, and held it up.

'Now, if you press the bit of plastic rubber against this,' he explained, 'the finger print can be produced the right way round. It's quite easy.'

The jury found him not guilty. The prosecution, of course, had had no opportunity of cross-examining him, and apparently the jury thought there was an element of doubt. What does that mean? Clearly that they thought the police might have put the man's finger print on to the bottle. Consider the questions that he might have been asked.

'Did the police take your finger prints on plastic rubber? Or on plaster? They took them on smooth paper, didn't they? How would they transfer that to a bottle? Why do you carry that plaster cast of a finger print? When did you make it? Whose finger print is it? You agreed that they should take your finger prints when you were charged? You were told you could refuse?'

In the *Journal of Criminal Law and Criminology,* published by the Northwestern University Press of Chicago, November-December, 1934, there are two articles about the counterfeiting of finger prints. In one of them Dr Harold Cummins of the Tulane University of Medicine describes how he made finger prints in some plastic dental impression compound by using plaster cast dies. The prints were indistinguishable from others made by actual fingers. He then got a commercial engraver to make a zinc plate from a natural finger print. With this he made a 'negative' in dental wax, and from the negative a cast was made on a film of gelatine. He stuck the gelatine film on to a dummy finger (also made of gelatine)—and made perfect finger prints.

Then he tried out his forgeries on a team of eight finger print experts. On a sheet of cardboard he impressed four prints of the same right index finger, two of them made naturally and two by the dummy finger. The experts knew that some of the prints were genuine and some forgeries, but they had to say which was which.

Only two of the eight experts got all the answers right. Five of them got one or more mistakes. Out of the total of thirty-two answers, twenty were right, eleven wrong, and one doubtful. The experts more often said that genuine prints were forgeries than *vice versa*. In a further test there were six other experts—one of them a police officer in charge of a finger print bureau. The results were roughly the same.

You have to remember that in both these tests the experts were actually *looking* for forgeries which they knew to be there—and the prints were nice, clear impressions in rolled ink. 'The results,' says Dr. Cummins at the end of his article,

> point against acceptance of the common dictum that a counterfeit finger print would be inevitably recognised as such.

And a footnote to the article says that Dr Erastus Mead Hudson, of New York,

> has devoted special attention to the subject of finger print forgery during a period of some fifteen years.

Experimenting with methods of forgery, he is convinced that counterfeit prints can be made with such success as to defy detection.

So is Professor Charles Sannie, head of the Criminal Identity Department of the Paris Prefecture de Police. In 1955 he told a meeting of the International Criminal Police Commission ('Interpol'), at Istanboul, about the case of a prisoner serving a sentence who put his own finger prints on a piece of glass and gave the glass to someone paying him a visit. The visitor smuggled it out and later left it at the scene of a burglary—which took place while the owner of the prints was actually in prison with the tightest of all alibis. To meet the growing ingenuity of the finger print forgers, Professor Sannie urged an extension of the 'Bertillon finger print system', which combines anthropometry with finger prints; but nothing can change the fact that the anthropometric part of the system comes into operation only after you have caught your man.

The same article in the *Journal of Criminal Law and Criminology* contains an article by Captain C. D. Lee, of the Police Detective Department, Berkeley, California, who says:

It is with considerable reluctance that finger print experts have come to realise that finger prints can be forged, and to have to admit as much when testifying in Court.

There is always, accordingly, the possibility that finger print experts may be called for the defence; and if the technique of forgery makes any considerable headway, we may in time see forensic battles about 'loops and whorls' as erudite at the psychiatric jousts that worry juries today ('Members of the jury, the prisoner's case is that this finger print is a clever forgery. He was never at the scene of the crime at all.') Certainly the likelihood is not that criminals will arrange to leave about the finger prints of their accom-

plices, but that they will 'develop' and plant those of
innocent and law-abiding persons; and while this would
involve small risk of identification as an offender with a
'record,' it might put an innocent person on his defence and
involve him in worry and cost. The man with the bad
record, whether innocent this time or not, would of course
have infinitely greater reason to worry.

We might therefore see Finger Print Consultants opening
offices in the same spirit as Income Tax Recovery Agencies;
the private detective, after a century of colourful work for the
prosecution, emerging from the pages of fiction to help the
defence (Entrust Your Alibi to Us: Finger Print Forgeries
Exposed: etc.). A case at the Old Bailey foreshadowed
some of this twenty-five years ago. In September, 1931, a
woman called as a witness in a prosecution was being cross-
examined as to her character, by way of showing that she
was not a witness of reliability or truth.

'Is it right,' counsel asked her, 'that in 1927 you were
convicted, with a man known to the police as a criminal,
of stealing?'

After a short, incredulous silence, she became so genuinely
indignant that the judge intervened.

'That is quite untrue, is it?' he asked her.

'It's absolutely monstrous,' she said. 'What right have
they to say such a thing?'

'No doubt you are prepared with proof in the usual way?'
the Judge said to counsel. At that time, proof 'in the usual
way' would be the production of a record of the woman's
conviction plus merely the evidence of a police officer that
she was the person described in it. This could quite easily
fail to expose the fact that an instance of totally mistaken
identity was now taking place. Only one way is known, at
the moment, of refuting such 'proof,' and that is the use of
finger prints; but in this case it was the accused person, and
not the accuser, who invoked them.

'You can take my finger prints,' she said. 'That's the

way the police reckon to prove this sort of thing. Take
my finger prints.'

And they did. She adjourned to the police room; finger
printing apparatus was hurriedly brought from Snow Hill
Police Station, across the road; and when she was duly
'printed,' it was shown beyond doubt that she was not
the woman counsel had been told she was. The defence
had made a serious blunder, and yet the belief as to
this quite innocent woman's identity must have been
strong.

Finger prints are occasionally discussed in the High Court,
usually in the course of actions against the police for
damages for unlawful arrest. If a man unlawfully arrested
is 'subjected to the indignity of having his finger prints
taken' (it is always called an indignity, though he can refuse
to have it done—in England but not in Scotland—if he
doesn't like it), it always appears to increase the enormity
of the injustice done to him. It may even be good for
another £50 damages.

On 19th September 1942, a Liverpool ambulance atten-
dant, in uniform, was cycling home from his depot after a
day's duty. It was half past ten at night. Two policemen
stopped him to tell him that his rear lamp was not alight,
and then they noticed that he was carrying a loaded sack on
the frame of his bicycle. 'What's in there?' one of them
asked. He told them the sack contained soap-flakes, which,
although he was unaware of it, were at that time a rationed
commodity. 'Where did you get them?' came the inevitable
and policemanly question.

'I got them from my mate,' he said. 'He's one of the
regular drivers at the hospital garage.'

'What's his name?'

(There was a dispute in the case as to whether he said
the driver's name was Appleton or that he didn't know the
name.)

c

'Where does he live?'

'I don't know.'

'Well, we'll come back with you to the garage and see if we can find him.'

Again, some dispute in the evidence: the police said that he invited them to go to the garage, while he said that they took him there. If they took him there, from that moment, whether the two policemen would have thought so or not, he was under arrest. If he was in fact at that moment 'unlawfully in possession of property which there was reasonable ground to believe or suspect had been stolen,' they were entitled, under the Liverpool Corporation Act, 1921, to demand his name and address, and to arrest him if they were not forthcoming. Up to that moment, they rather suspected that he was in possession of rationed goods for which he had not surrendered 'points'; but this, although it was a war-time offence, would not have justified the subsequent charge. They also suspected, naturally enough, that those rationed goods were stolen, but they had not yet made sufficient enquiry to justify arrest on that ground. Already then, in all probability, he was unlawfully arrested.

But as they approached the garage he showed signs of nervousness.

'Look here,' he said, 'my mate's not on duty.'

It takes less than this to transform a policemanly suspicion into a moral certainty. One of the policemen, having asked the prisoner only for his name, not his address, went into the garage and asked if the driver was on duty. He was not; and with no more enquiry the prisoner was taken to the police station and charged with unlawfully having in his possession about fourteen pounds of soap flakes. It was a Saturday night. He was released on bail, and on the following Monday he was remanded for two days at the request of the police—again on bail—for further enquiries. On the Wednesday the police had to say that they had no further evidence to offer. The case was dismissed and he was discharged 'without a shadow of reflection on his conduct or character.' It was an almost perfect case for an action against the police.

The action came on at Liverpool Assizes before Mr Justice Lewis, who took the view that the policemen were justified in making the arrest under the Liverpool Corporation Act, and added, in effect, that the arrest would have been justified by the Common Law even if the Liverpool Corporation Act did not exist. So he dismissed the plaintiff's action; and the plaintiff promptly appealed to the Court of Appeal in London.

The Court of Appeal decided that the Common Law did not support such an arrest, since the suspicion that the man had committed a felony (i.e. *stolen* the soap flakes) was not reasonably founded; and anyway, the court added, the police had made no attempt to plead that it did. 'The police had failed to make such enquiry, from either the plaintiff himself or those at the garage, as would entitle them to think they had reasonable grounds for suspicion.' The court allowed his appeal, awarded him all his costs against the police, and sent the case back to the Assizes for a new trial that was to concern itself solely with how much money he was to get in damages.

But the interest of the case, for present purposes, lies in what Lord Justice Scott had to say in the Court of Appeal about the taking of finger prints. 'There is, I believe,' he said, 'no statutory sanction for the practice disclosed in the present case of the police taking finger prints of a person under a charge before he is convicted or even committed for trial.

Such treatment is inconsistent (he went on) with our British presumption of innocence until proof of guilt: and it is natural for it to be regarded as a slur on a

man's character. Without free consent it involves trespass
to the person; and following upon an unjustifiable arrest,
it may become an element in the false imprisonment, and
be properly taken into account on the assessment of
damages . . . If it be a common practice to take finger
prints before committal or summary sentence, I venture to
think that it deserves consideration by the Home Secretary
in consultation with the Lord Chancellor.

Now this is odd, because the police, in England, never
take the finger prints of a person in custody—or of anyone
else—without his consent, and always tell him that he is
entitled to withhold it. If he asks about the consequences
of refusing, they may tell him (or they may think it a good
idea not to tell him) that the magistrate will be asked to
remand him in custody because 'their enquiries are not yet
complete;' and that once he is at the remand prison his
finger prints can be taken by force. (I don't know whether
this is ever done, but imagine that it could sometimes be a
messy operation, culminating in black finger prints on the
faces, throats, collars and clothing of half a dozen exhausted
officials.) Moreover, in this case as in so many, it was the
taking of the finger prints that enabled the police to find out
quickly that the prisoner was a man of good character. The
charge, and the painstaking course of police enquiries, might
have overshadowed his life for quite a long time in the
days before finger prints were used as a means of establishing
identity. And from the public policy point of view, a police
rule that finger prints must not be taken, even with consent,
would ensure that most of the hardened criminals were
always treated as first offenders; while countless innocent
persons, circumstantially but wrongly suspected, would have
to forego permanently the vindication that finger prints
can so often ensure, and innumerable cases would remain
for ever in the statistical column known as 'not cleared
up.'

If this worries you, some reassurance is to be found in the Scottish case of *Adair v. McGarry,* since any real conflicts between the Scottish and English legal systems tend to be resolved sooner or later if they involve questions of individual liberty, and the view of the Lord Justice General seems rather the more sensible:

> It is beyond all doubt (he said) that provided a person has been legally arrested by the police, they may examine his person and his clothes for blood stains and the like, or for any mark on his person which, according to their information, was observed when the crime was committed— without his consent and without any magistrate's warrant. Every man is entitled to the enjoyment of personal liberty, but he forfeits that right by committing crime. And where the criminal law warrants his arrest on a criminal charge, his personal liberty is unavoidably invaded, not merely by subjecting him to detention, but also to the extent necessary to enable the police to observe and collect the real evidence (afforded by his person, his apparel, or the contents of his pockets) of his connection with the crime and his identity with the criminal.

No doubt the Lord Justice General would have wide support when he said that a man forfeits his right to the enjoyment of personal liberty by committing a crime; but the problem of pre-trial procedure in general, and finger printing by the police in particular, is that the person being detained and finger printed may be totally innocent of any crime. You must, however, regard every suspect as a person whose liberty is already abridged for the moment, and balance his rights and liabilities in the way described by Lord Sands in the same Scottish case:

> Finger print taking being a new thing (he said), there can be no Common Law rule upon the particular matter any more than there can be a Common Law rule as to

whether a man may be X-rayed without a warrant who is suspected of having swallowed a watch or a coin. In balancing the two considerations, facility in the detection of crime on the one hand and the rights and liberties of the citizen on the other, we must have a sense of proportion. Is taking a man's finger prints in the like category to examining his arms for tattoo marks, or making him don his cap or his overcoat for an identification parade, or, on the other hand, is it a serious invasion of his person or liberty, such as detaining him without any warrant beyond what is necessary, or shaving off his beard? As it appears to me, the taking of a man's finger prints falls clearly within the former category.

It is less than ten years since the 'charge sheets' used at police stations provided columns headed Hair, Eyes and Complexion. These were filled in, as a rule, just after the charge had been read out to the accused person; and the process involved a cursory inspection of him from the neck upwards, by a constable acting as a kind of gaoler, who would call out to the station officer doing the writing, with an inevitability that seemed to show that heads were far more alike than finger prints: 'Brown—grey—fresh, sir.' Some hardened and cheerful prisoners would call it out for themselves. There was also a column headed 'Particular Marks on Person,' or, in more laconic instances, 'Marks'. This would seldom contain anything more intimate than 'mole left cheek,' 'freckles' or 'scar over right eye', and it would not assert 'boil on neck' unless the boil looked like lasting a very long time. It had been known to include 'broken nose' and 'prominent Adam's apple,' but these were instances of an uncommon devotion to duty. It all lasted long after the development of the finger print system, and was discontinued, in different parts of the country, as different Chief Constables accepted the view that a man's finger prints distinguish him more reliably than brown—grey—fresh. But

the two things overlapped for forty years; and it is probable
that they still do it somewhere.

How much less offensive was this than taking a man's
finger prints? and doesn't the comparison remind you at
once that brown—grey—fresh would never help in establishing whether the arrested man had ever been at the scene
of a crime? Lord Sands had something interesting to say
about that too:

> A man has been arrested on suspicion of a crime where
> finger prints were left. Now I understand that an officer
> with an expert eye, looking at the man's finger tips
> through a hand glass, could tell (not indeed accurately,
> but with sufficient confidence to determine that it would
> be justifiable to detain or release the suspect) whether
> his finger tips corresponded with the photograph of the
> print left on the window pane. Nobody, I think, will
> question the legitimacy of looking at the suspect's fingers,
> and requiring him to hold them up for that purpose. But
> it is said that one must not, without a warrant, adopt the
> much more satisfactory course of taking an impression,
> to ascertain whether there is any ground for detaining the
> man. This seems to me unreasonable.

When he spoke of 'requiring' a prisoner to hold up his
hands, Lord Sands must have contemplated that a man who
refused to hold them up would have them held up by the
police. Indeed, he went on at once to deal with the question
of compulsion:

> Another agument which has been suggested is that no
> man can be compelled to supply evidence against himself.
> Now, if the man voluntarily gives his finger prints no
> question arises. The sole question relates to compulsion.
> If a man's finger prints could not be obtained without
> some voluntary action on his part, and were to be obtained
> only by tormenting him until he agreed to give them,

I could understand the argument. . . . An Ephraimite who was compelled at the point of the Gileadite's sword to pronounce the word 'Shibboleth' might perhaps have complained that he was compelled to incriminate himself. But not so the man whose finger prints are forcibly taken. He is entirely passive, and is not compelled to do anything by an exercise of his own will or control of his body.

And in the American case of *The People v. Sallow,* Mr Justice Wadhams said this:

No volition—that is, no act of willing—on the part of the mind of the defendant is required. Finger prints of an unconscious person, or even of a dead person, are as accurate as those of the living. By the requirement that the defendant's finger prints can be taken there is no danger that the defendant will be required to give false testimony. The witness does not testify. The physical facts speak for themselves: no fears, no hopes, no will of the prisoner to falsify or exaggerate could produce or create a resemblance of his finger prints or change them in one line, and therefore there is no danger of error being committed or untruth told.

None, indeed. But from the viewpoint of the prisoner who does not like incriminating himself, the danger doesn't lie there. It lies in the probability that error will be avoided and the truth laid bare. I hope it is possible to say without disrespect that some of these judicial pronouncements reveal a high degree of occupational speciousness. If the prevalent system of identification required that the accused person should strip and stand on his head instead of merely surrendering the control of his hands for five minutes, similar arguments could be used to show that he was not being required to supply evidence against himself. The case against any inherent right in the police to take finger prints

by compulsion could be argued, line by line, against most
of the passages I have quoted here. But in England they do
not need to be argued: the assumption is that to take the
finger prints of a non-consenting person would, so far as the
police are concerned, be an assault and a trespass to the
person unless the policeman doing it had the authority of a
magistrate. And the fact has been recognised by section 40
of the Magistrates' Courts Act, 1952, under which an order
can be issued by the magistrates in the following terms:

IN THE COUNTY OF

....

PETTY SESSIONAL DIVISION OF

....

BEFORE THE MAGISTRATES' COURT SITTING AT

....

———————

William Brown (hereinafter called the defendant)
having on the 10th day of March 1956 been taken
into custody, is this day charged that he on the 8th
day of March, at........................ in the County
aforesaid, did steal a bicycle: and application
being made to the Court in that behalf by Police
Inspector Thomas Jones of the........................
Police Force:
And it appearing to the Court that the defendant
is not less than fourteen years of age:
It is ordered that the finger prints of the defendant
be taken by a Constable.

And taken they are, either at the court, or at a remand prison, remand home, police station or other place to which he goes whether in custody or on bail. 'And a constable may use such reasonable force,' says section 40, 'as may be necessary for that purpose.'

English distaste for the whole business of finger prints, except in the crime news and in detective stories, is deep seated and eloquent. They will not have finger prints on birth and marriage certificates, wills, pay sheets, post office savings bank books, pension documents, or on documents like the identity cards that they had to carry during the war. On November 17, 1937, Mr Rupert de la Bère asked the Home Secretary in the House of Commons whether he was prepared to consider the national registration of finger prints throughout the country, so that they could be filed away for use by the police in tracing unknown persons suffering from loss of memory. 'With other people unidentified as the result of accident or otherwise,' said Mr de la Bère, 'there are said to be over 9,000 such persons in asylums, hospitals, and other places in Britain.' The answer given by Mr Geoffrey Lloyd, the Under-Secretary, was the one that has been given many times before and since. 'The Home Secretary,' he said, 'would not feel justified in considering the question of a national finger print registry for the purpose indicated, unless he were satisfied that there was a real and general desire for such a system.'

No Home Secretary need ever fear that such a demand will, suddenly or gradually, force itself upon him. It must be one of the delights of running a democratic country that whenever you are asked to do something adventurous, irksome, or too remote from what was done last time, you can demand proof of a public demand, although you can clap rates and taxes on without the bother of a door-to-door popularity poll.

With a national finger print registry there could have been

no Tichborne Case. No Adolf Beck, no Oscar Slater would have suffered from the certainty of so many witnesses that he was somebody other than Adolf Beck or Oscar Slater.

Neither, when you come to think of it, would you be reading this book.

VI

THE IDENTITY
OF ADOLF BECK

'**T**HAT is the man—I should know him anywhere.' The more confident this assertion sounds, the more it must remind anyone within earshot of the tragic case of Adolf Beck. This was a man who in 1896, on the evidence of at least ten different women, was sent to penal servitude for seven years for a series of frauds committed by another man. The fact that Adolf Beck was entirely innocent was not established until long after he had come out of prison; but if his case is pre-eminent among stories of mistaken identity, that is because it is the most documented and written about. It could always happen again.

On 16th December, 1895, Adolf Beck came out of his lodgings at 139, Victoria Street, London, to buy an evening paper. In the gathering dusk he stood for a moment on the threshold. A woman stepped across to him and laid a hand on his arm. 'I know you. I know who you are.'

He drew back. 'What? Who are you? I'm sorry, madam, you are mistaken.'

'I should know you anywhere.'

'What is it you want from me?'

'Want from you? Why, I want my two watches and my rings.'

Beck had no idea what she meant. She was a complete stranger to him. What was she—a prostitute, a decoy, someone trying to embroil him in a dispute, with accomplices watching and ready to demand hush-money? He was a man

76

with associations of the kind that the police, almost wistfully, call 'undesirable' when they not merely fall short of the specifically criminal but involve women. In the few seconds that it took these ideas to prompt a course of action, he had made the decision which, though it was natural enough, lent unfortunate weight and colour to the accusations that were to follow. He ran away.

He ran across Victoria Street and then half-ran, half-walked until he saw a policeman on duty by the clock-tower at the corner of Vauxhall Bridge Road. By the time he reached the constable, the woman had caught up with him.

'This woman,' he told the policeman breathlessly, 'has accosted me. I don't know her! I don't know what she wants——'

'Don't you mind what he says,' interrupted the woman. 'He stole two watches and some rings from me, and he also gave me a forged cheque for £40. I want to give him in charge.'

A constable is bound, by the powers and duties he has inherited from his Common Law ancestry, to take into custody anyone who is credibly and reasonably accused, by some apparently responsible person, of having committed a felony. Stealing watches and rings, forging cheques—these are felonies. The woman making the accusation, Miss Ottilie Meissonier, a German-born music-teacher living in Putney, seemed entirely respectable and convincing. If the accusations were unfounded it was she, if anyone, who would be liable to damages. 'Will you come to the police station with us, madam, and make these charges formally?' asked the policeman. She would indeed. So off to Rochester Row police station went this quite typical trio, Miss Meissonier walking on one side of the policeman and the incredulous and indignant Mr Beck on the other.

The story she told at the police station was one that she manifestly believed herself, and was sufficiently circumstantial to 'identify' Mr Beck as the thief and forger she declared him to be. Among the events *subsequent* to a crime that are said to afford evidence of the criminal's identity, it will be remembered, is the fact that the accused person tried to run away. In Mr Beck's case, as it turned out, to get clean away and never again be traced would have been the one and only chance open to a totally innocent man. However, once a 'reasonable' probability of suspicion has been set up at the quasi-judicial enquiry in a police station, all the accused person's protestations of innocence are likely to be treated as matters he should bring to the notice of the magistrate in due course. If a serious mistake has been made, it is the mistake of the person preferring the charge, upon whom all the consequences must fall: the function of the police, they are able to remind themselves comfortingly, is executive, not judicial. There are cases in which an experienced station officer, long emerged from the hag-ridden juniority in which every entry he makes in 'the books' is assumed by his superiors to be probably wrong, rejects the charge and tells the accuser that if he still wants to proceed it is open to him to ask a magistrate to issue a summons. (This is, indeed, possible in every kind of case in the criminal calendar, a fact that is too little known.) But Mr Beck was put in a cell; and a little later he was 'put up for identification' (see Chapter III) in order that he might be seen by two other women from whom someone, in precisely similar circumstances, had stolen jewellery and obtained other goods on the strength of a forged cheque. They both said that Mr Beck was the man: they would 'know him anywhere.'

At this time Adolf Beck, a Norwegian by birth, was a man of forty-four. As a youth he had been a merchant seaman, though he was an educated man with a training in chemistry. He landed in Cardiff when he was twenty-four, and began a series of employments with ship's chandlers and brokers in Bristol, Cardiff, Liverpool, Aberdeen and

Glasgow. In 1868, unable to settle for long, he went to South America, where he earned his living again in ship's brokers' offices but also had considerable and slightly incongruous periods of professional singing on the concert platform and in grand opera. From 1874 until 1884 he was in Peru, earning large sums through contracts for the supply of food to the troops engaged in the Chile-Peruvian War— he had become a 'financier' under the influence of the famous 'Colonel North.' And he came back to England in 1885, to begin a series of copper-mining speculations in which he showed a neat grasp of the less lovable artifices invented by the bogus company promoter of the period. But by 1890 he was borrowing half crowns from his friends, and moving from one hotel to another on a descending plane of respectability.

The importance of that brief biographical note is that it accounts for Beck's whereabouts in the year 1877, the middle of what we could call his South American period. But let us return now to Rochester Row Police Station and the accusations of Miss Meissonier. She told a story which, in its exact similarity to the stories told by scores of other women who later came forward, affords ludicrous proof of the average criminal's slavish devotion to any routine that has once proved successful. She had met a man (she swore it was Adolf Beck) in Victoria Street about three weeks before—a man stopped her and asked if she was Lady Everton. No? Must be somebody else. They 'got into conversation.' She was going to a flower show at Westminster. Oh, but why? said the man. It was such a poor show. Now, he had flower gardens on his Lincolnshire estate that were looked after by ten gardeners; yes, she said, she had some very nice chrysanthemums at home. Indeed? Might he come and see them? He might, and did the next day. By this time he was a man with an income of £180,000 a year, a cousin of Lord Salisbury's, and the owner of great estates in London and the provinces. Would she come on a yachting trip to the Riviera? She would need some smart clothes, but he would buy these; and he rapidly made out a list of the creations she would need, telling her where to order them. She could start paying for them, he said, with a £40 cheque which he then made out on a non-existent account at the Union Bank in Trafalgar Square. And that jewellery wouldn't do, either—he would take the bracelet and get two black pearls put in it; he would also get her a better diamond ring and would borrow the one she was wearing in order to have the size of her finger. He arranged to have the glass in her watch mended, and he displayed such interest in a tiny antique watch she showed him that, although she had not missed it until he had gone, she had no doubt that it went with him. The other discovery she made after his departure was that the Union Bank had never heard of him. And the next time she saw him was outside his lodgings at 139 Victoria Street three weeks later. That was when she gave him into custody.

'I knew him at once,' she said. 'I should know him anywhere.'

Mr Beck, of course, denied the whole story strenuously. But there is only one answer to an accusation like this, only one way to side-step an irksome identity that looks like enveloping you by due process of criminal law. That is an alibi. But how many people can remember what they were doing three weeks ago, without some enquiry? And then of course there came a series of women to 'identify' him. First, Miss Meissonier's maid, Mary Harvey, who picked him out from a dozen other men in the parade room at Rochester Row police station without hesitation as the man she had admitted to her mistress's flat three weeks before, and whom her mistress had afterwards declared to be a thief. And this alone was enough, at that stage. He was formally charged with stealing Miss Meissonier's jewellery and forging a cheque for £40.

Then the police proceeded to call upon twenty-two other women who had been similarly victimised during the preceding twelve months to see whether they could identify Mr Beck as the offender. The stories they had told to the police varied little from that of Miss Meissonier; apart from the larceny of their jewellery and the passing of the forged cheque (which the man had usually put into a wax-sealed envelope that they were to hand in at the bank unopened), they had all been invited to become his 'housekeeper' in St John's Wood, and had all been assured that their renovated jewellery would be brought back to them by the Commissionaire from his hotel, who was a man with one arm.

'Identification parades' were staged at Rochester Row police station and elsewhere; ten of the women were absolutely certain that Beck was the man, picking him out easily. Eleven others were a little less sure. And one of them—according to the reports—was positive that he was *not* the man (though how this was discovered, since the suspect must in no circumstances be indicated to the witnesses, is not recorded). The ten confident ones went in due course to the Magistrates' Court to repeat their stories and identify Mr Beck with their traducer; and with the consequent reports in all the newspapers the first stage in his story of misfortune was complete.

Then, from under their stones, there came out as usual those writers of anonymous letters to the police who are stirred into life by every much-publicised crime. One of these reminded the Commissioner of Police that the charges in the case of Adolf Beck bore a striking resemblance to the crimes of a man calling himself John Smith, who was convicted at the Old Bailey eighteen years before of robbing numerous women, and was sentenced to five years' penal servitude. John Smith and Adolf Beck, it said, were probably one and the same person. It has never been published, but it was probably signed Pro Bono Publico.

There would be less scope for such a letter today. If John

Smith were convicted nowadays, his finger prints would remain in the Criminal Record Office at New Scotland Yard, and Adolf Beck's finger prints, taken at Rochester Row police station on his arrest, would irrevocably dispose of any suggestion that the two men were identical. But in 1895 there were no finger print records; and what is more, there was no register of criminals grouping them according to their 'modus operandi'—as to which, this narrative now makes a short digression.

The Criminal Record Office at New Scotland Yard keeps a number of indexes to known criminals, apart from the main finger print register. One of these is the Modus Operandi Register, and it is based on the curious fact that most criminals not only stick to one kind of crime but usually repeat the same methods in committing it. So the Register has a Method Section, and that Section has a Fraud Index, classifying all the known tricksters according to the particular story which they always repeat, with the most fatuous regularity and self-confidence, to their victims. The method used by the real thief in the Adolf Beck case, for instance, was ludicrously identical in relation to each one of the defrauded women. Each woman was accosted in the street (and the full reports of the case make it clear that some of them were the kind of women who hoped to be accosted); the same day or later there was an assignation at the woman's flat, when the story of great wealth and estates was convincingly told; the offer was made and (impliedly, at least) accepted that the woman should become the man's mistress at an address in St John's Wood; there was the gentle criticism that her clothes and jewellery were below standard; there was accordingly the 'borrowing' of the jewellery for improvement or replacement, and the order on some well-known shop—it was usually Redfern's—for an impressive list of new clothes; there was the worthless cheque, sealed and not to be opened, with which the woman was to start a banking account; there was even the 'borrow-

ing' of a few shillings to pay the man's cab fare back to his
hotel; and there was the final assurance that the new or
repaired jewellery would be brought to the woman by a
hotel commissionaire with one arm. Why one arm? Simply
because the story had always succeeded and there was no
need to cast about for fresh little touches of verisimilitude.

Today, in view of the massive and minutely sub-classified
card index of the Modus Operandi Register, a criminal who
works so rigidly to pattern might as well leave at the scene
of each crime his name and address, with an indication of
the hours at which he is most likely to be at home. But he
still does it, supplementing his finger print file with the
further details that, among all the burglars with broken
noses or left feet that turn in, he is one of the smaller
company that uses a candle, feeds the dog, cuts the telephone
wires, uses a brace and bit or leaves by means of a rope.
(Or it may be the other way round.)

Today, the anonymous letter about Adolf Beck would
have been superfluous. But that does not say that his case
might not have been linked up with John Smith's. As it was,
the 1877 'papers' about John Smith's case were got out, and
a handwriting expert declared that Smith's handwriting and
Beck's were identical, though Beck was now writing in a
disguised hand. Moreover, the police officers who were
concerned in the 1877 case, and who were now living in
retirement, were called into counsel and both said that Beck
was the man they remembered.

The evidence was now overwhelming. Beck was committed for trial at the Old Bailey, on an indictment that
charged him with numerous cases of larceny (which is a
felony) and false pretences (which is a misdemeanour) and
also alleged that he was similarly convicted in 1877 in the
name of John Smith. Before the trial began Mr Horace
Avory (later Mr Justice Avory), who appeared for the
Crown, decided to drop all the charges of larceny, because
he thought that all the watches and jewellery had been

obtained by false pretences. In this he is now generally
considered to have been wrong, since the essence of the
misdemeanour known as 'obtaining property by false
pretences' is that the victim shall have parted with the
ownership as well as with the custody of his property,
relinquishing, in response to the false pretence, all expectation of its return. None of the women had done this, and
their property had therefore been obtained from them by
larceny, the possession being secured by trickery. But the
elimination of all the larceny charges from the Beck indictment, which left only misdemeanours, raised a new problem.
Under the Prevention of Crimes Act, 1871, it was quite
proper that the indictment should contain an allegation that
Beck had a previous conviction, in 1877; one of its purposes
being to subject him, in the event of conviction this time,
to a period of 'police supervision' on discharge from prison.
But Avory, apparently overlooking this provision, seems to
have thought that the position was governed by an earlier
Act that forbade the mention of previous convictions except
where the indictment was for felony. He therefore removed
from the Beck indictment all mention of the 1877 conviction, thus, with the best of motives, depriving Beck of
his main defence.

That defence, which was in the hands of Mr Charles Gill,
Q.C., was to be that Miss Meissonier and all the other
women in this case had been defrauded by the man who
committed the 1877 crimes—and that this could not be
Adolf Beck, who at the time of these crimes was in South
America. Avory's action in dropping all mention of the
1877 crimes from the actual indictment set Gill casting about
for some other way of getting them mentioned in Court.
He asked the Common Serjeant, Sir Forrest Fulton, who was
trying the case, to send the jury out of Court while he made
a submission on the point: it was vital to his case.

'My Lord,' said Mr Gill when they had gone, 'it is a
strange situation, but if I am not allowed to raise this

question of my client's supposed conviction in 1877 as John Smith, I cannot call evidence of his absolutely complete alibi in relation to that offence.'

'What is the alibi?' asked the Common Serjeant.

'That Mr Beck, my Lord, was in South America throughout the time that John Smith, whoever he is, was committing these offences and serving a five-year sentence for them.'

'And how do you propose to introduce the subject before the jury?'

'I hoped to cross-examine the handwriting expert, my Lord, who says that these two men are one and the same person, and then call my South American alibi witnesses to show that what he says cannot possibly be true.'

Sir Forrest Fulton turned to Horace Avory.

'What does the Crown say to that, Mr Avory?'

'I should object to that, my Lord. It is a collateral issue. It should not be enquired into until after the jury have returned their verdict, lest it should be afterwards said that the prisoner was improperly convicted.'

'I should like to hear you on that, Mr Gill?'

'It's a question directly in issue, my Lord,' urged Gill. 'I am entitled to raise it. My case on behalf of the prisoner is that the man convicted in 1877 is the man who has been committing these frauds, and that the prisoner has been mistaken for that man. My client desires to show, by cross-examination, that the writing of the man convicted in 1877 is the same as that of the exhibits in the present case.'

'It would be an unusual way of disproving a previous conviction,' said the Common Serjeant, 'especially when it is not even before the jury. You have to put it in yourself in order to destroy it?'

'Exactly, my Lord. There is now no other course open to me. But upon this question of the value of the handwriting expert's opinion, I am entitled to have all the documents produced which have been submitted to him. They include the 1877 documents.'

The Common Serjeant pondered.

'Have *you* anything to add, Mr Avory?'

'Only that I object, my Lord, to the witness being asked whether these exhibits are in the same writing as the lists of clothing and jewellery in the present case. That, in my submission, could only be taken by the jury to mean that the prisoner committed the crimes of 1877, and the jury ought not to be allowed to hear a word about it.'

'I am obliged to you both,' said Sir Forrest Fulton. 'I rule against you, Mr Gill. The question whether the prisoner is or is not the man convicted in 1877 is not admissible, because it relates to another and distinct issue, and one which is calculated to mislead the jury. If witnesses are to be called as to the prisoner's good character, then of course Mr Avory may choose to cross-examine and show, by putting this conviction to them, that the prisoner's character has been bad. Or he may choose not to have the issue confused by the introduction of that matter. I say nothing about that. But I cannot have this question of a previous conviction introduced in any irregular way. Let the jury be brought back into court.'

That was the end of all hope for the defence. It meant the complete collapse of Gill's case. The South American witnesses were there, to prove that Beck was a well-conducted resident in South America for seventeen years, amply covering the whole period of the 1877 crimes and of John Smith's sentence. But to the jury, who knew nothing of what had happened in 1877, this would merely mean that he had not been in trouble before; and although that inference fully entitled Avory to call evidence to show that he had, he refrained from motives that were ironically well-intentioned. Moreover, in those days no prisoner was allowed to give evidence on his own behalf, though the law was altered in that respect only two years later. So the end was certain. Adolf Beck was found guilty, and Avory rose once more to address the Common Serjeant.

'My Lord, the police are in possession of certain information with regard to the prisoner.'

But no: not even now was this growing tragedy of errors
to be arrested.

'I don't think,' said the Common Serjeant, 'that I should
be influenced by anything that they might be able to tell
me.'

And having thus killed the last chance by which Beck
might have cleared his name, he turned to the prisoner.

'Adolf Beck,' he said, 'you have been found guilty of a
most base and wicked crime. You have heartlessly robbed
these persons, relying on the fact that, having regard to
their previous history, they were not likely to bring the
matter before a public court. The sentence of the court
is that you be kept in penal servitude for seven years.'

A prisoner in an assize trial has always seemed to me
the extreme instance of depersonalised misery, a lay figure
symbolising all the ways in which human identity can be
translated from a privileged and dignified possession into a
burden and an affliction. In those days the practice of the
courts ranked him rather lower. Even so, on a felony charge
Beck would have been perfunctorily asked 'whether he had
anything to say why the court should not give him judgement
according to law?' But he stood convicted only of
misdemeanour: a mere seven-year sentence should not call
for any particular remonstrance? He was not asked to say
anything; but he burst out, nevertheless, with the words
that many a guilty man has used in the Old Bailey dock,
before and since:

'From the beginning to the end of these horrible charges I
have had nothing whatever to do with them. I am absolutely
innocent.'

And it was absolutely true. But he was taken away to serve
his seven years' sentence. During his years in prison he
petitioned the Home Secretary sixteen separate times to
have his case reconsidered; and every one of his petitions

was rejected. Many guilty men, of course, protest their innocence to the last, and many, too, petition the Home Secretary for redress, retrial, unconditional release, and so forth. But it is not often that a petition is rejected when positive proof is forthcoming that the petitioner is an innocent man. This is what happened in the case of Adolf Beck.

In Wormwood Scrubs Prison he was given the convict number worn eighteen years before by 'John Smith,' with the addition of a letter to show that he was no longer a first offender. After nearly three years his solicitor, who was still worried about the case and had already handled some of his many petitions to the Home Office, discovered that the real John Smith was a man named Wilhelm Meyer, and that he had been in London throughout the trial of Adolf Beck, The important part of this discovery was that Wilhelm Meyer was known to be a circumcised Jew. On this information the Home Office at last had enquiries made, and it was found that the prison records showed John Smith, alias Wilhelm Meyer, to be circumcised, and that this important distinguishing characteristic was never known either to the police or to the Public Prosecutor. It was easy enough to establish then that Beck was not circumcised.

So he was released? On the contrary, the Home Office said that the 1896 evidence against him was so overwhelming that the new evidence about his identity was irrelevant. All they did was to give him a fresh convict number and stop thinking about his aliases. And thus it went on for another three years, Beck sending petitions to the Home Office whenever he could get his way with a perplexed and exasperated Prison Governor. Years later it transpired that the Home Secretary himself, Sir Matthew White Ridley, never saw one of them.

In 1901 Beck was released, on what was then called ticket-of-leave. He threw himself into the job of proving his innocence. He got his story into the newspapers, and George

R. Sims wrote a series of rhetorically sentimental articles about him. The Salvation Army helped him generously. He spent hundreds of pounds in his campaign. And then suddenly, in 1903, there was another outbreak of exactly the same kind of frauds on 'women of the town.' John Smith was at work again. The police, at once suspecting Adolf Beck, arranged for some of these women to watch him entering and leaving a café that he was known to frequent; and they all swore again that he was the man. Again he was arrested and charged.

This time, at the Old Bailey, the judge was Mr Justice Grantham, who seems to have had one ear attuned to the mundane affairs that go on outside the temples of justice. Beck was again convicted, despite the fact that this time, under the Criminal Evidence Act, 1898, he was able to give evidence on his own behalf; and this time of course his previous 'convictions' were proved in court, but the Judge postponed sentence until the following session in order that some more enquiries could be made.

How far those enquiries were in fact pursued is imperfectly recorded; but on July 7, 1904, only a day or two before Beck was to come up again for sentence, the elusive John Smith himself was at last arrested, still pursuing his chosen career of defrauding women in just the same way as ever. He was arrested in the act of pawning some rings he had just obtained from one of them; he had given her a list of the clothes she would need to become his mistress, handed her a cheque in a sealed envelope, borrowed the rings to get them repaired—all the familiar steps in this never-failing swindle, this perfect example of the criminal's well-known devotion to an undeviating *modus operandi;* every detail of each crime almost laughably the same.

At about midnight he was sitting in a cell at Tottenham Court Road police station when Inspector Kane, of the Criminal Investigation Department, paid a routine visit to the station, read in the station books the story of John

Smith's arrest and the description of his methods of fraud, and went to the cells to have a look at him. The story of Adolf Beck's first trial and his much-publicised protestations of innocence, even if they were now beginning to fade from the public mind, had been revived by his new appearance at the Old Bailey; but in the mind of Inspector Kane, who had been in court through both trials, the facts were particularly clear because he had always felt that there might indeed have been an injustice. He had, perhaps, some experience of identification parades and their unexpected consequences. He decided to find out everything he could about John Smith—incidentally devoting the whole of his leisure hours to the enquiry, led on by the growing and exciting certainty that he had discovered the existence of a great wrong, and that now, after all this time, only he would ever take the trouble to expose it. He had a short conversation with John Smith, who had given no address and was 'not talking'—and he got nowhere. He therefore set about getting the newspapers interested in the case, so that the next morning's court proceedings should be widely reported. The result was one of those fortunate instances wherein the Press reports of court proceedings, which often obstruct what is known as the course of justice, actually smooth it. People who read about John Smith's activities came forward with evidence about him, and Inspector Kane in a very short time got the address of his lodgings—which, lawfully or not, he promptly searched without a warrant. He found plenty of evidence that John Smith was Wilhelm Meyer, the man convicted in 1877.

John Smith was committed for trial, and Adolf Beck's case was again 'put back' to await the new developments. On 15th September, 1904, Smith came before Mr Justice Phillimore at the Old Bailey, pleaded guilty to charges of stealing rings from three women, *and admitted his conviction for the similar offences in 1877*. Mr Charles Matthews, who appeared for the Director of Public Prosecutions, made a long statement completely vindicating Adolf Beck and showing him to have been twice convicted, and once heavily punished, for crimes of which he was completely innocent. John Smith had nothing whatever to say about his conduct, or about the cynical indifference with which he had seen an innocent man serve a long prison sentence for crimes he had himself committed. Mr Justice Phillimore gave him a richly-deserved homily and five years.

Adolf Beck was then given what the law so oddly calls a 'free pardon'—it is only the law that pardons you for what you have not done. He was also awarded £4,000 compensation, which was roughly £500 a year for the whole of the time he had been in prison, on remand, serving sentence, or on ticket-of-leave. It is hard to resist the conclusion that this contemptuous award reflected some official disapproval of the women in his life. (After all, if a man will go with these people . . .) But the probability is that whatever he got would have had a short life: within five years, a destitute man, he died of pleurisy in Middlesex Hospital.

Meanwhile, moved at last to action by a sustained campaign in the Press, the Home Secretary had appointed a committee of enquiry comprising Sir Richard Henn Collins, (the Master of the Rolls), Sir John Edge (a former Chief Justice in India), and Sir Spencer Walpole. Its secretary was the Hon. Malcolm MacNaghten, who later became Mr Justice MacNaghten. Its report was sharply critical of the Home Office for its apathy and half-heartedness, mildly disapproving about the Common Serjeant for his conduct of Beck's first trial, and tactfully corrective about Horace Avory's presentation, as Treasury Counsel, of indictments that involved previous convictions. Some of the leading figures in this legal imbroglio attacked each other in letters to the newspapers; and no one admitted that, from first to last, he had done anything wrong.

The whole case imparted a final spurt to the movement

for establishing a Court of Criminal Appeal, which came into being three years later—greatly reducing, but by no means destroying, the chance that a Beck case could ever happen again.

To look at the photographs of these two men now (they are reproduced in *The Trial of Adolf Beck,* Notable British Trials Series, William Hodge & Co. Ltd.) is to wonder that either could be taken for the other; and your astonishment increases as you study the descriptions taken from their prison medical records. When it has been said that both had 'oval faces,' were about 5ft. 6in. in height, and were proportionately built, the normally visible similarities are complete. But Beck's complexion was fresh and Smith's dark; his eyes blue and Smith's brown. Beck had a small mole on the right side of his neck and a scar on the left cheek. Smith had neither of these, but he had scars on his lower lip, on his nose, and on his right jaw. Their voices may have seemed similar, for Smith, though English-born, was of Austrian Jewish parentage and was taken as a child to live in Vienna, where he acquired a teutonic accent, while Beck's Norwegian accent had never left him. But there the resemblances end, leaving the observer, at this distance of time, with the uncomfortable reflection that accusation can always be nine points of conviction. As a parable on the insecurity of personal identity, the case of Adolf Beck combines the tragedy of a cruel injustice with the quality of Gilbert's mockery in *Cox and Box*: 'Have you a strawberry mark upon your left shoulder?' 'No.' 'Then you are indeed my long-lost brother.'

VII

THE IDENTITY
OF OSCAR SLATER

A MAN once recommended to me, as a cure for insomnia, a mental exercise that kept me wide awake for four nights. 'Imagine,' he said, 'that you are unjustly accused of having murdered someone three months ago exactly. Circumstantially, the case against you is absolutely complete, and yet you are innocent. Do you admit that such a thing is possible?' I knew that it was, and said so. 'Then instead of counting sheep,' he said, 'try to work out what you were doing on the the day of the murder, and what witnesses you can call to prove it. If you keep on reminding yourself that you are faced with a murder charge, it's wonderful the way it keeps your mind on the job. What sends you to sleep is the concentration of thought on a hopelessly elusive purpose.' What I did find was that by establishing salient points of recollection—a journey, a party, a theatre, an illness—you could get much nearer to the actual date than you might suppose; but I never once established a single fact about the vital date itself. It was the implications of all this that kept me awake.

In the year 1912, Lieutenant John Trench, of the Glasgow City Police, was sent to Broughton Ferry, in Forfarshire, to investigate a murder case. An old lady who lived alone had been found clubbed to death in her own home, and there were a number of 'witnesses' who had seen a strange man loitering near the house on the day of the crime (there always are). The description they gave, which varied widely as such eye-witness descriptions usually do, had been supplied to the police authorities throughout Great Britain. It happened that an Australian ne'er-do-well named Charles Warner, who was then serving a sentence of fourteen days in Maidstone Prison for vagrancy, seemed to the Kent police to be rather like the man described. They notified Lieutenant Trench, and he took five of the 'witnesses' on the long journey South to see Warner 'put up for identification.' All five picked him out (from among eight other prisoners) without hesitation. It is said that one woman was in tears as she exclaimed: 'I know I am putting a rope round his neck, but that is the man.'

Warner denied that he had ever been to Scotland in his life, and swore that he had never heard of Broughton Ferry or the murder of the old lady. But Lieutenant Trench could do no other than arrest him, and back to Scotland the whole party went. There, at further identification parades, twelve more witnesses 'identified' Warner, and he was charged and remanded.

He then did what it is so often impossible to do, and was possible in his case precisely because he belonged to the class of globe-trotting vagrants who so often come into conflict with parochial laws: he remembered where he was on the day of the murder—he was in Antwerp. Lieutenant Trench, told of this, went to see him in prison—Trench, it appears, was for some reason uneasy about the identity of his prisoner; and at that interview Warner suddenly remembered that on the day of the murder he had pawned a waistcoat with an Antwerp pawnbroker. This was a miraculously lucky transaction for Warner: he had 'slept out' in Antwerp, and had no way of proving his movements by reference to the registers of hotels or common lodging houses. The next day Lieutenant Trench left for Antwerp.

He found the pawnshop without difficulty. The waistcoat was still there; and it had been pawned on the day of the murder. Meanwhile the Procurator-Fiscal in Scotland had taken statements from over a hundred persons, and the case against Warner was being formidably built up. With the return of Lieutenant Trench from Belgium it totally collapsed, and Warner was released.

That experience in the career of Police Lieutenant Trench was to lead, indirectly, to his dismissal from the Glasgow City Police in 1914 and to further misfortunes which must have made him wonder, at times, whether human identity is capable of any verification at all. For John Trench was one of the Glasgow police officers involved in the famous case of Oscar Slater in 1908—Oscar Slater who was mistakenly 'identified' by a large number of witnesses as the murderer of an elderly lady, was convicted on the majority verdict of a Scottish jury, sentenced to death, reprieved, and kept eighteen and a half years in prison before his innocence was established—established largely through the persistence of Trench himself. Trench never had any doubt that Oscar Slater was wrongfully convicted, and for years after Slater had gone away to prison he was worried by the fact that evidence he himself had obtained during the police investigations, deeply implicating a well-known person who was never charged, had been suppressed by senior officers of the Glasgow City Police. Oscar Slater, a man of known bad character, was the man of their choice and they were determined that he should be convicted. It was not until March 1914, five and a half years after the murder, that Trench's disclosure to a solicitor was made public—and he was promptly dismissed for communicating police information to persons outside the force.

But first let us recapitulate briefly the facts of Oscar Slater's story, which would still seem incredible if it were not that recent years have produced cases uncomfortably similar in detail and consequences.

Oscar Slater was a German Jew. His real name was

Leschziner and at the time of his trial he was thirty-seven. He was a much travelled man—all parts of Europe and the United States had at various times sustained him in his alternate roles of bookmaker's runner, gambler, 'dealer' (omnibus word!) street-market jeweller, and ponce. He arrived in Glasgow in 1894, took a hand in the economics of that city's prostitution trade, and in 1901 married a girl named May Curtis. He parted from her after four years; and it seems likely enough that his intense desire to stay apart from her, and nothing else, accounts for the stealthy movements that he was later so tragically unable to explain away—including his use of many aliases. Then he met Andrée Antoine, a girl of 23, at that famous rendezvous, the Empire Theatre in Leicester Square, London; and he lived with her for the next three years in London, Paris, New York and Brussels, coming to Glasgow in November, 1908, to rent a flat at No 69 St George's Road—and to buy and sell jewellery, gamble, drink and loaf.

In a first-floor flat round the corner from St George's Road, at No 15 Queen's Terrace, West Princes Street, lived Miss Marion Gilchrist, a spinster of eighty-three. She lived alone, on a small inherited income, and assiduously collected antique jewellery—which she kept in extremely vulnerable places in her flat and which was said to be worth, at the material time, about £3,000. There was no evidence that she knew Oscar Slater or that he knew her. But she had a maid, Helen Lambie, who was 'walking out' with a young bookmaker; and since there *was* evidence that Helen had told him about the jewellery, its presence in the flat could easily have become known among the bookmaking circles frequented by Oscar Slater.

Old Miss Gilchrist liked to see who was coming up the stairs from the street door before she decided whether to come out of her flat. When someone rang or knocked at the street door, she could open it by means of a lever inside the flat; then she could come out and tell the visitor at the open door below to come straight up, or, if she disliked the look of him, hurry back into the flat and shut herself in. After that, you would get no response unless you knew the particular signal that gained admission for trusted visitors. In the flat below (No 14) lived Mr Arthur Adams (a musician aged forty-four) with his mother and five sisters; and this family understood that if ever the old lady wanted urgent help she would knock loudly on the floor three times.

At seven o'clock on the evening of Monday, December 21, 1908, the Adams family suddenly heard three loud knocks on the floor above. Arthur Adams ran to the street door and found it open. He hurried up her stairs and three times rang the door-bell of the flat, violently, peering through the glass panel of the door. He heard what he thought was a sound of 'breaking sticks.' He waited a minute and a half, heard no more, assumed that the maid was 'doing up her kitchen,' and went back to his flat downstairs. One of his sisters made him go up again—'she thought there must be something wrong.' He was just ringing the door bell again when Miss Gilchrist's maid came up the stairs from the street—she had in fact been to buy an evening paper for her mistress.

'Here,' he called, 'there's a strange noise in your house— the ceiling's been like to crack.'

'Oh,' she said, 'that would be the pulleys—the clothes-airer in the kitchen.'

'I'll just wait and see if everything's all right,' said Mr Adams.

She unlocked the door with her key, just as a man appeared in the hall of the flat, coming from the spare bedroom. He walked coolly past the maid 'with his head down,' past Mr Adams—and then (Mr Adams told the police later) he went down the stairs 'like greased lightning' and banged the street door.

The maid's conduct at that moment is interesting and

D

significant. She showed no surprise at the man's presence; and once he had gone, she went calmly to the kitchen to examine the pulleys of the clothes airer, apparently to see if they were in fact noisy. Then she went into the spare bedroom from which the man had emerged, because it was unusual for it to be lighted. And then Adams called out to her.

'Where's your mistress?'

She turned and went into the dining room.

'Oh!' she screamed. 'Oh! Come here!'

Adams ran in. Miss Gilchrist lay on the floor near the fireplace. Every bone in her face and skull had been smashed, her breast bone and ribs were all broken, and there was blood on the fireplace, the coal-scuttle, the fire-irons, and parts of the wall to the height of the overmantel. The old lady was not quite dead—she lingered, unconscious, until they had brought a policeman on to the scene at twenty minutes past seven.

In the spare bedroom a wooden deed-box had been wrenched open and its papers scattered about the floor. Lying untouched on tables were a diamond and two rings, a gold bracelet, a gold watch and chain, and half a sovereign.

The maid said that the one thing missing was a crescent-shaped diamond brooch that was usually in a small dish on the dressing table. All the rest of the old lady's jewellery, worth about £3,000, was intact.

And at this point I quote, with the permission of his publishers, the conclusions of Mr George Wilton Wilton, B.L., formerly Sheriff Substitute for Lanarkshire, who has studied the case from the viewpoint of one with a lifelong interest in finger prints:

From beginning to end of the trial, and throughout the proceedings in the appeal, no one engaged in the Case, at the Bar or on the Bench, ever raised—even out of curiosity—any question over the absence of any search for finger prints, whether relevant or not to the prosecution, the defence, and the conviction of Oscar Slater, or to success in his appeal.

Impressions of hands and fingers of the murderer of Miss Gilchrist must, it is thought, have been made on the disturbed wooden box, its papers, the furniture, and other articles about the rooms and hall, as well as on the window-panes and door-handles of the house, besides the banisters and walls of the common stairs. It is improbable that on some of these places her assailant left no fingermarks, blood-stained or otherwise. Such marks may or may not be visible to the naked eye; some may be latent on glass and even on material such as cloth, and these can be discerned and 'developed' only by finger print experts.

So far as I can find, not one of the members of the Criminal Investigation Department of the City of Glasgow Police, from the Superintendent downwards, seems to have thought of directing attention to or looking for finger prints.*

Mr William Roughead says, in his Introduction to *Oscar Slater* in the *Notable British Trials* series,* that 'the case occurred before the days of finger print tests, for the application of which the circumstances of this crime afforded ample opportunity.' He had in his possession, he said, a photograph of Miss Gilchrist's fireplace, 'showing the blood-splashed grate, together with the celebrated chair,' on the back of which was plainly to be seen the imprint of a hand—possibly bloody. 'Had modern scientific methods been then available,' wrote Mr Roughead, 'this should have settled the question once for all.'

* *Finger Prints: History, Law, and Romance*, by George Wilton Wilton. Hodge (1938). Pp. 164–5.
* William Hodge & Co. Ltd., 1929.

The 'celebrated chair' was a small, ordinary chair standing near Miss Gilchrist's body, with its left leg soaked in blood and the inner face of both front legs blood-splashed. The doctor called to the scene concluded that the attack was made with the chair itself, by someone standing over the prostrate woman and hitting down with great force. The doctor thought this would account for the apparent lack of blood on the murderer himself (neither the maid nor Mr Adams had noticed any blood on him, and there was never any evidence that Oscar Slater got rid of any blood-stained clothing) because the seat of the chair would act as a shield to the assailant.

But there is no record that this chair was ever examined for finger prints. The chair does not seem to have been so much as considered by anyone else as the probable weapon; once the experts came into the case, the chair went out of it. Why, it seems quite impossible to say. Mr William Roughead was mistaken, moreover, when he wrote that this was 'before the days of finger print tests.' A man was convicted of burglary, on the evidence of one thumb print, at the Old Bailey on 13th September, 1902;* and thereafter not a year went by without the conviction of criminals on finger print evidence—notably in the City of Bradford, which established the first provincial finger print bureau in 1903. And at the time of the Oscar Slater case in 1908, everyone must have known of the notorious trial, three years before at the Old Bailey, of the Stratton brothers, who were convicted of murder and executed on the evidence of the finger prints one of them had left on the inside tray of a cash-box.

'The Scottish police,' says Wilton in his book on Finger Prints,† 'lost a great opportunity over the Gilchrist murder case. If finger impressions of her assailant had been obtained, I agree with Mr Roughead that their use then "should have settled the question once for all." What tragic consequences

---

* *Scotland Yard*, by George Dilnot. Geoffrey Bles, London, 1929.
† *Op. cit.*

to Slater and to other individuals ensued through the strange
failure to search for finger prints?'

They were more tragic for Slater, of course, than for
anyone; but among the 'other individuals' for whom they
were also tragic was Police Lieutenant Trench, who paid a
heavy but by no means unusual penalty, years later, for his
attack on the probity and efficiency of his colleagues and his
superior officers.

There was the customary list of people—about a dozen—
who had been in West Princes Street, outside Miss Gilchrist's
home at various times during the previous three weeks, and
had seen 'a man walking past,' 'a man loitering about,' 'a
man looking at the house.' He had a moustache; he was
clean-shaven; he looked foreign; he looked British. At five
minutes to seven on the evening of the murder 'he' was
standing against the railings outside the house. 'He had a
long nose, with a most peculiar dip. You wouldn't see that
dip among thousands' . . . This was better—it was one of
Mr Adams's sisters speaking. He had a clean, clean-shaven
skin and was very dark, with high cheek-bones; and he wore
a brown overcoat and cap.

But the man who came out of the old lady's flat a few
minutes later, leaving her dying on the floor, passed the
maid and Mr Adams in the doorway and ran down the
stairs, was wearing 'a light coloured overcoat and a cloth
hat' (according to the maid) and 'seemed gentlemanly and
well-dressed' (according to Mr Adams). Some of the statements made to the police, as usual, turned out to be lies—
their authors' motives varying from exhibitionism to the
sudden idea that to have been near the scene of the crime
at a given moment would furnish an alibi or excuse for some
quite trivial embarrassment of their own. Out of a welter
of conflicting personal descriptions, the Glasgow police
selected a couple that might do and 'circulated' them. And
on Christmas Day, 1908, a Glasgow cycle-dealer named

McLean went to the police and told them that a man named 'Oscar,' well known to him because they belonged to the same club, had not only been missing since the murder—he also had a long nose with a dip, or slightly twisted to one side, and he had been asking people to buy a pawn ticket for a diamond brooch said to have been pawned for £50 on the day of the murder.

The police went after 'Oscar' in full cry. They soon discovered, from his club and his bookmaker confrères, that he had a number of aliases, that the brooch had absolutely nothing to do with Miss Gilchrist's missing one, that for at least a couple of weeks before the murder he had been telling people that he was shortly going to San Francisco, and that on Christmas morning he had told two woman friends (they knew him as Oscar Slater), when they arrived to take over his flat, that he was 'going to Monte Carlo for three weeks.' And off he went, with his mistress Andrée Antoine, destination in fact unknown.

The police could no longer rely on the brooch to connect him with the murder. What other links were there? His false names; his 'sudden' departure from home (they seem always to have regarded this as sudden, though he was a lifelong nomad and had, weeks before, given people his proposed San Francisco address); his varying statements as to where he really was going; the fact that he lived only just round the corner from Miss Gilchrist; and his rather long nose that had once been broken. But above all, far above all, the fact that he lived with (and inferentially, lived on) a prostitute, who according to their maid, 'received gentlemen friends and went out to the music halls.' He had gone to America, said this maid, not to Monte Carlo: she had been told to say it was Monte Carlo, and she supposed it was because he wanted to evade his wife.

In fact Oscar Slater and Miss Antoine were by now on the *Lusitania* as 'Mr and Mrs Sando,' on their way to New York. A cablegram was sent to the New York police asking

them to detain 'Otto Sando second cabin Lusitania wanted
in connection with the murder of Marion Gilchrist at
Glasgow.' He had a twisted nose, it added. And it requested
that he and Miss Antoine should be searched for pawn
tickets.

A case that may not seem very convincing in discussion
takes on a most heartening verisimilitude when you begin
condensing its salient features into cablegrams. And yet,
significantly enough, two days *after* that cablegram went
to New York the Glasgow police published (for the first
time) an offer of £100 reward to anyone who could give information that might lead to the arrest and conviction of
the murderer.

When Oscar Slater and Miss Antoine were arrested and
searched on the *Lusitania*, there of course was the pawn
ticket for the diamond brooch which, as everyone now knew,
had no connection whatever with the murder. Slater and the
woman violently protested that they had never heard of Miss
Gilchrist and knew nothing of the crime. (Most people did
know about it, and they were perhaps protesting too much.)
Still protesting, they were taken off the ship and into custody
—he to the Tombs Prison, she to Ellis Island.

Now there seems absolutely no doubt that they were both
entirely innocent of any complicity in this murder. But the
machinery of the law was now in operation, laboriously
setting the stage for what was to become a classic illustration
of the fact that, in matters of personal identity, accusation
can sometimes be nine points of conviction. Extradition
proceedings were brought before Mr John A. Shields,
United States Commissioner for the Southern District of
New York; and the witnesses as to Oscar Slater's identity,
specially brought from London to give evidence, were Mr
Adams (the occupant of the flat under Miss Gilchrist's), the
maid who had found the old lady dying, and a little girl
who said she had seen a man running away from the old

lady's house but who, it later transpired, was lying to account for being late home that evening. One circumstance in the whole incredible case that may seem most difficult of all to believe is that before the extradition proceedings opened, these three witnesses *actually saw Oscar Slater being taken along a corridor of the building, handcuffed to two officials of the court*. Years afterwards, one of these two officials gave evidence at an enquiry that he had heard Mr Charles Fox, counsel for the British government who was presenting the demand for extradition, say at that moment in the corridor to the two girls: 'That's the man.'

As if this were not enough to reduce any subsequent 'identification' to absurdity, Mr Adams and the child had been shown photographs of Slater before they went to the court. In the court, Oscar Slater sat with his attorney, where anyone would expect to see him; and the three witnesses all remained in court to hear one another examined and cross-examined. When they were asked if they could see him in court, they all pointed at him!

But the evidence proved unexpectedly long-drawn-out. Counsel on both sides, it seemed to Slater, made the utmost of every opportunity to stall, object, delay, and adjourn. New documents, depositions, and even witnesses were sent for from Scotland. At last, on 2nd February, 1909, when the case had been going on for exactly a month—and Miss Antoine had been a month on Ellis Island—Slater decided not to contest the proceedings further, to return to Glasgow voluntarily, and there to vindicate himself in a legal atmosphere that he would be more likely to understand. (After all, if he won the extradition proceedings, he would still be for ever debarred from returning to Great Britain unless he was prepared to face the music.) 'I shall go back to Glasgow with my free will,' he wrote from the Tombs prison to a friend in Scotland, 'because you know so good than myself that I am not the murder. . . . You know the best reason

I have left Glasgow because I have shown to you the letter
from St Francisco from my friend, also I have left you my
address from St. Francisco . . . They only have taken the
statements against me and not for me. Likely I will be in
Scotland in 14 days and so quicke that you hear that I am
in prison in Glasgow send me the best criminal lawyer up
you get recommendet in Glasgow. Keep all this quiet because
the police is trying hard to make a frame-up for me.'

As indeed they were, ably abetted by the press and by
most of Slater's former 'friends'—the recipient of this letter,
for example, took it straight to the police. The blood-hunt
was on: everyone wanted Slater. Slater was their man, the
gambler, pimp, and 'dealer.' While he was still in New York
a Glasgow private enquiry agent (engaged and paid by
whom—an anonymous well-wisher, a newspaper?) had come
to certain conclusions that involved someone very different
from Slater. He went with his discovery to Glasgow City
Police Headquarters, and was told to mind his own
business. Thereafter, perhaps, he was taken care of by
the Scottish prosecuting system, the law of libel—and the
police.

The Anchor liner *Columbia* arrived at Renfrew on
21st February, 1909, with the unfortunate Slater on board.
As he went to the head of the gangway to leave the ship,
a member of the crew kicked him.

On the very day of his arrival Slater was again 'put up
for identification,' and one of the police officers present
at this function was Lieutenant John Trench. When he gave
evidence about it later, he did so in an atmosphere created
by several other witnesses who had said that of the eleven
people called in to make up the identification parade nine
were policemen, that there were only three or four people
in the room anyway, that some of them looked foreign, that
none of them looked foreign, that they all resembled Slater
and that none of them resembled Slater—and that all the

witnesses had seen photographs of Slater at one time or another. In view of all this, his answers to Mr A. L. M'Clure, K.C., who represented Slater at his trial, are of special interest to anyone interested in problems of identity.

'Were there any foreign-looking men among them?' asked Mr M'Clure.

'No,' said Trench, 'they were all Scotsmen, I think.'

'No one of dark complexion and foreign appearance?'

'There were some of them of dark complexion.'

'And foreign appearance?'

'No, not foreign.'

'So that anybody looking for a foreigner would, of course, go straight to the prisoner?'

'Possibly, yes.'

It seemed almost as fatuous as what had happened in New York. That 'possibly, yes,' ought to have ended the case, in the absence of better evidence; and the rest of the evidence was worse. Mr M'Clure went on to question Lieutenant French about the Glasgow police practice in arranging identification parades.

'That is rather an irregular way of conducting an identification, is it not?'

'I don't think so,' replied Trench, and it probably wasn't at that time.

'But I understood,' said Mr M'Clure, 'that when you were going to identify a person in connection with an alleged crime you attempted to get him placed amongst men who were more or less like him. Isn't that so?'

'No,' said Trench, 'it isn't.'

'But just as a matter of ordinary fairness, don't you think that would be a proper practice to observe?'

'It might be the fairest way, but it is not the practice in Glasgow.'

Times have changed. It is the practice now. I take the following passage from *The Scottish Police, an Outline of*

Their Powers and Duties, by James Mill, City Prosecutor, Edinburgh : *

> Wherever possible, at least four persons other than the accused should be paraded along with him. These persons should be of similar height, build, and general appearnce —e.g. clean shaven or otherwise, as the case may be. Their clothing should be similar to that worn by the accused—or, at least, not noticeably different; e.g. it would be improper to parade the accused in an overcoat and all others without one; or that the accused should wear a cap and all others soft hats. If the accused has some marked peculiarity—e.g. bright red hair—individuals with a similar peculiarity should be selected.

In other words, you should aim at a general resemblance. Lieutenant Trench was actually asked whether any of the people paraded did resemble Slater.

'Oh no,' he said, 'none of them resembled Slater.'

'And Slater's photograph, as an obvious foreigner, had been published in the Glasgow evening papers before that?'

'Yes,' said Lieutenant Trench; and there were witnesses who said that the police had actually shown them photographs of Slater, and *then* asked them if they could pick him out from among the people paraded. Mr James Mill's *The Scottish Police* has good advice to offer here, too:

> It is pointless to bring to an identification parade a witness to whom the police have previously shown a photograph of the suspect, as must sometimes be done— e.g., to enable a warrant to be applied for. The best procedure is to show the photograph to one only of a number of available witnesses, to apply for a warrant to arrest on the strength of his photographic identification, and to summon to the parade staged after arrest only those witnesses to whom a photograph was not shown.

* W. Green & Sons Ltd., Edinburgh, 1944, p. 95.

Should the case go to trial, the witness who saw the photograph will, of course, be asked to identify the accused in court.

It seems incredible today that Slater should have been found guilty on such evidence, but found guilty he was, and sentenced to death. Within a day or two the police released for publication their own account of his past life, which, though involving only one minor conviction (for fighting in the street), was a somewhat revolting *dossier* of mainly un-proved allegations of immorality. One effect of its publication was that while a petition for Slater's reprieve was being canvassed for signatures, one of the tables set up by a canvasser in Gordon Street, Glasgow, with ink and writing materials, was smashed by a mob. And when the reprieve was announced, the police made certain of im-mortality for their own share in the case by issuing, or at least authorising, a public statement of indignation.

For the story of Sir Arthur Conan Doyle's long campaign to get Slater's conviction quashed, and the venomous opposition he aroused in the respectable newspapers, one should turn to Mr William Roughead's famous account,* and to an excellent later book, *The Great Suspect,*† by Mr Peter Hunt. It will be sufficient to say here that the evidence accumulated by Conan Doyle, by Police Lieutenant Trench, and others kept the case intermittently alive for nineteen years—long years for Slater, in Peterhead Prison—and resulted at last in an extraordinary and, so far as I know, unique Parliamentary decision. Largely because of Slater's case, a Court of Criminal Appeal had been established for Scotland in 1926; and in the following year, Parliament retrospectively authorised it, by means of a rushed-through single-clause Bill, to review the trial of Oscar Slater—who had, as it happened, just been released on licence from

* *Trial of Oscar Slater*. Wm. Hodge & Son Ltd. 1950 Ed.
† Carroll & Nicholson, 1951.

prison. It quashed his conviction. And after a month or two more of inelegant wrangling and stalling on the part of the Government, he was awarded £6,000 compensation.

And what of Police Lieutenant Trench, the one man who had told Oscar Slater's judge and jury how absurd an identification parade really was, who said in court that to place the prisoner among men 'who were more or less like him' was an idea that 'might be the fairest way, but was not the practice in Glasgow'? His activities on behalf of the wrongly convicted man entailed accusations against his superior officers in the Glasgow City Police, a course which has an easily predictable end. After his dismissal he joined the Royal Scots Fusiliers, and on May 13, 1915, was just about to sail with his regiment for the Dardanelles when he was arrested by his old colleagues on a totally misconceived charge of receiving stolen jewellery! He stood in the very dock where Oscar Slater had stood six years before, heard the Lord Justice-Clerk tell the jury that there was no justification whatever for the charge, and was released immediately. The moral of his story is that, once a series of witnesses have committed themselves to a positive statement on a matter of personal identity, they can seldom be shaken, and once their evidence has been sanctified by judicial acceptance, it is highly dangerous to question it further. Cross-examination may discredit such witnesses, but they will then begin to lie. Among the seventy-four witnesses who gave evidence against Slater there must have been many liars, even if some of them achieved a kind of self-redemption by coming to believe their own lies as the case dragged on. Lies were piled upon lies until the whole miserable edifice reached the Secretary for Scotland, the Home Office in London, Parliament and the responsible newspapers. No one knew the truth—except, I think, Miss Gilchrist's maid, who unfortunately kept quiet even when the Scottish Court of Criminal Appeal, after nineteen years, quashed Slater's conviction. Detective-Lieutenant John Trench, who did not keep quiet, paid a penalty that was only less than Oscar Slater's. I have seen it happen elsewhere . . .

I do not recommend, as a soporific, the line of thought described at the beginning of this Chapter. I offer on the contrary a counsel of perfection: two valuable aids to the good life are available to the man who keeps a careful and exact diary: one is sleep, and the other is the blessed solitude of personal identity.

VIII

EMERY,
THOMPSON AND POWERS

IT is clear enough, as I write, that whatever changes may hereafter take place in the law of homicide in this country, one of the last offences to be taken out of the category of capital crimes will be the murder of a police officer. The use of the death penalty for this offence seems still to command wide assent. But by greatly reducing, during the past one hundred and fifty years and in particular the last five, the types of murder so punishable, we have increased rather than lessened the emotional and ethical need for supreme care in guarding against errors of identity in the few instances that remain. The death penalty for killing policemen will probably seem indispensable so long as we do retain it, and it imparted a special poignancy to the case of Emery, Thompson and Powers.

These three men, Leonard Richard Emery, a street trader, James Edmund Powers, a van driver, and Arthur Joseph Thompson, a baker and street trader, were criminals (or at least, former criminals), known as such to the police. Being known to the police is a status that confers, in practice, a kind of second-class citizenship, the main characteristic of which is an enormously and painfully enlarged personal identity. If you are a well-known burglar, car-thief, or shop-breaker, your whereabouts will be among the current news that is of interest to the constabulary, so that you will be given unlooked for opportunities of explaining to them where you were last night, and why.

*   *   *

111

On the night of 16th October, 1953, these three young men sat drinking tea in an all-night 'transport café' on the Great West Road at Brentford. Outside they had parked a black Wolseley car; and the time was 3.30 a.m. Those circumstances form an almost classic combination in the anatomy of modern crime, and the three men were, as I have said, already known criminals. At half past three two policemen, in plain clothes, came into the café and spoke to them. 'I thought they wanted to look in the car because it was so late at night,' Powers said later. 'But then they told us we resembled three men who had attacked a police officer at Marlow; and we had to go to Brentford police station with them.' They were at Brentford police station for some hours, giving separate (but reasonably identical) accounts of their recent movements. They had all been enjoying the hospitality of a Mr and Mrs Bloomfield, friends of Emery's, at Ashford, in Middlesex, whither they had gone at 10.10 p.m. 'to discuss a coal contract'—a cartage job, you and I might call it. They had called at the café on the Great West Road on the way home at about 3.15 a.m. Powers was seeking to purchase a lorry for the compendious purpose known as 'general dealing.' It does not seem to have been possible, at that stage, to bring forward any witnesses to identify them as the men who had attacked the policeman: so they were allowed to go—not on bail, for they had not been charged and could not be required to give any such undertaking, but in an atmosphere that suggested a merely temporary parting. One police officer seems to have told them that it 'might well end in a murder charge'; and he might well have been proved right.

Three days later, they were all arrested again, this time at their own homes—Emery at London Road, Ashford, Thompson at York Road, Wandsworth, and Powers at Dempsey Close, Virginia Water. They were told that they had now been identified as the three men who had attacked Police Constable Cecil Pye, of the Bucks Constabulary, at

High Street, Marlow, at 1.30 a.m. on the night of 16th
October, 1953. They all strenuously denied any knowledge
of the attack, but this time they were formally charged with
'causing grievous bodily harm' to the policeman.

The rest of this story and its implications cannot be
fully savoured unless it is made clear at this point that all
three were later proved to be completely innocent of that
charge.

Let us now turn, therefore, to what had happened on the
relevant night at Marlow, in Buckinghamshire. At 1.30 in
the morning, Police Constable Pye of the Bucks Constabulary left the police station to patrol his beat, and fresh
in his mind was an 'Information Room' message from New
Scotland Yard that Emery, Thompson and Powers were
known to be on their way to Bucks in a Wolseley car to
commit a crime. As the young constable turned from High
Street into Institute Road, he heard a noise that seemed to
come from the rear of the 'Corner Café.' He went into the
side turning to investigate. As he got nearer he saw two
stationary cars, a 'Standard' which was usually parked there
all night, and a black 'Wolseley' which was a stranger. (This
later turned out to have been a 'Jaguar,' but the police
message had required him to look out for a Wolseley with
three men in it.) He was shining his electric lamp on the
'Wolseley' when, again, he heard the slight noise, and
this time realised that it came from behind the 'Standard.'
Moving his light quickly, he saw a man crouching by the
car. As the light fell upon him, this man leapt to his feet,
grabbed a broken kitchen chair that had been lying nearby,
and brandished it above his head; and then, just as the
policeman saw that there were two other men, the first one
threw the chair at him. It missed him, and the other two
advanced upon him with golf clubs held above their heads.
The policeman backed away, shining his torch in their
faces to dazzle them; and back in the High Street, he turned
and ran for the nearest telephone box—it was outside a Post

Office. Hearing the two men running after him, he pulled out his truncheon as he ran; and halfway between the corner of Institute Road and the telephone box, he glanced back to see the two men still after him with the golf clubs raised.

One of them, he later swore, was Thompson, though Thompson was, in fact, at that moment sitting in the Bloomfield's house at Ashford. The curious feature of the whole case and its bearing on the problem of identification is that the men were afterwards known to have been wearing nylon stockings over their faces.

Just as the constable tore open the door of the telephone box, one of the men struck him on the head. He struck back with his truncheon, but failed to land a blow. 'I felt blood streaming down the left side of my face,' he told the magistrates, 'from a cut above my left eye. The men were trying to prevent me from telephoning, but I touched the emergency button. I was hit many times while I was outside the kiosk, and also inside. I remember being on my hands and knees outside the kiosk and hearing a car approaching. I thought: "Thank God, it's the police." '

But it was not. It was the black Wolseley (Jaguar) car again. It stopped by the kiosk, and the two men beating the policeman ran to get in. Then one of them (this was said to be Emery, who was also then drinking tea at Ashford) turned back to rain a few more blows upon the now prostrate policeman, who shouted: 'No more, no more—I've had enough.' Then the car, with the three men in it, drove rapidly away.

Most of this was witnessed by a Mrs Eileen Brown, who lived nearly opposite the Post Office in Marlow High Street and was awakened from her sleep by the noise of running and shouting. She got out of bed, and from the window of her third floor bedroom she saw the whole attack. Two other women in nearby houses were able to give the same kind of evidence: and so was Mr Peter Haley, at No 46, who hurried out into the street, found the badly injured policeman still trying to telephone for assistance, and took him indoors for 'first aid' treatment.

The policeman was soon afterwards hurried to the High Wycombe War Memorial Hospital, and found to have numerous lacerations of the skull and face, which necessitated forty-six stitches; and when the scene of the attack was searched by the police, they found that one of the golf clubs, a steel-shafted brassie, had been broken by the force of the blows and the pieces left lying near the telephone box.

Those two versions of the story did not come to be compared until the three men, Emery, Thompson and Powers were on trial on 25th January, 1954, before Mr Justice Stable and a jury at Northamptonshire Assizes (after a preliminary appearance at Aylesbury Assizes, whence the trial was transferred for reasons of speed and convenience).

The men were charged in an indictment under Section 18 of the Offences Against the Person Act, 1861, which alleged that they had 'caused grievous bodily harm to Police Constable Cecil Pye with intent to maim or disfigure him.' They were lucky not to be charged with attempted murder. Prosecuting counsel told the jury that 'these three men came down from London in the middle of the night, to Marlow, a peaceful little town on the banks of the Thames, for some purpose which we cannot prove. Do you think,' he asked the jury, 'they were there to see the beauties of the town by moonlight? Or were they there for some unlawful purpose?'

The story began, he said, on 14th October, when they hired a car from a firm near Staines. He described the policeman's discovery of the three men behind the Corner Café at Marlow, and their attack upon him. 'While the constable was in the kiosk they battered him with the golf clubs until one broke. It may be that one of the men then picked up the policeman's truncheon, for that has not been found. . . .' In fact it was ascertained long afterwards that the assailants not only had his truncheon but beat him with it. 'Then Powers drove up in the car, Thompson got inside, but Emery was not content with what he had done. He went back and had another go. Whether it was a kick or a weapon that was used is not known, but it is known that there was this other attack by Emery.' Counsel went on to say that at about 4 a.m., 'two and a half hours after the attack, the car which these men had hired previously was seen by police officers on the Great West Road at Brentford. It shouldn't have taken more than an hour to travel there from Marlow. What were they doing there in the meantime? I will tell you, members of the jury. They were taking care to fix themselves up with an alibi for that evening.'

(In reminding oneself, every now and again, that the three accused men were later able to establish their innocence, it is a piquant exercise in the uses of personal identity to imagine oneself in their place, listening to this long recital of allegations made against them by persons who utterly believed what they were saying was true.)

For reasons that have never been made public, there was no identification parade. Police Constable Pye gave evidence that he was shown by the police a number of photographs —'perhaps a dozen or more'—among which were those of Emery and Powers; and that he picked them out as his assailants.

The jury found all three guilty. Powers was then arraigned on a further charge of breaking into the house of Mrs Maud Janet Jones at Egham, Surrey, five days before the attack on the policeman, and stealing money and goods to the value of £282, and Emery on a charge of receiving a part of the proceeds of that crime. To this they both pleaded guilty. And Mr Justice Stable proceeded to deliver judgement.

'This form of thuggery,' he said, as Judges commonly do,

'is something which we will not tolerate in this island. Your record' (he turned to Emery, who had sixteen previous convictions, including one in the previous year for robbery with violence, who had twice absconded from approved schools, who had four times deserted from the Army, and who had already assaulted one policeman) 'is absolutely appalling. One faces a man in your situation with a feeling of absolute despair. You are a persistent and dangerous criminal. The sentence of the court is that you go to prison for ten years.'

Thompson was sentenced to seven years' imprisonment, and Powers to four.

It will perhaps be best for our purposes to see the rest of the story through the eyes of Thompson. His account, which was in the main corroborated by the other two and supported by witnesses, had been that on 15th October, 1953, he went to Newmarket races for the Cesarewitch. He won £130 on a horse called Chantry, and came back to London to 'celebrate in a pub in the Harrow Road.' He was still doing this at 10 p.m. when Emery walked in, accompanied by a man whom he introduced as Jimmy Powers, and said that he was negotiating for a coal delivery contract with the Co-operative Wholesale Society. 'I'm on to a good thing,' he said, 'but I need the capital to buy a couple of lorries.'

It occurred to Thompson that he had a brother-in-law, Leslie Mitchell, who was understood to have 'a couple of thousand pounds to invest.' They discussed an approach to Mr Mitchell, whose couple of thousand pounds was, in fact, the proceeds of a successful Court Action for damages arising out of a road accident at Nottingham in which he had received severe facial injuries. They then adjourned for the night.

The next day, Emery announced that there was a snag. He had already given the first option on the contract, he said, to a friend of his, Mr Bloomfield of Desford Way, Ashford. So that evening at about eight o'clock they drove out to have a talk with Mr Bloomfield and his wife at Ashford. There, Mrs Bloomfield (of whom not much is known except that she was a tireless maker of tea) said that her husband was out; and could they call back later? Then Powers suggested that they could fill in the time by going to look at a lorry for sale in Watford. On the way they stopped at two garages, ostensibly (and so far as Thompson knew) to buy petrol, but in reality, according to a later statement attributed to Emery, to size up one or other of the garages as a place to be robbed a few nights later.

Thompson always maintained that he knew nothing of any plan to rob garages until he learned of it in prison two years after his conviction at Northampton Assizes. In any case, the lorry at Watford proved unsuitable for their purpose, and they drove back to the Bloomfield's house at Ashford, arriving there (opportunely and significantly) just in time to hear the 'six pips' that preceded the radio ten o'clock news. Mr Bloomfield was 'still not home from work'; and this time they settled down to wait for him, playing cards and drinking innumerable cups of tea. They waited for five hours! And at the trial they were able to call a witness, an Ashford scrap-dealer, who had seen their car outside the Bloomfield's from 11.30 p.m. until after 3 a.m.

This must all have seemed as odd to the jury as to most of us, this driving about to inspect eligible lorries after dark, this sleepless card-playing in the small hours, in the house of a man whose wife would get cups of tea for them, apparently, all night. (When the police called to see her later that morning she showed them the cups still on the table.) At three o'clock, Thompson said he had waited long enough. So they went home? No: they drove to an all-night café on the Great West Road at Brentford; and when the police entered the café to question them (which is where we, too, came in) Emery and Powers were playing records on the juke-box. These two went outside for a 'quiet word' with one of the police officers, while the other officer said to Thompson: 'I understand you've been with these two men all night. I'm investigating an assault on a police officer at Marlow.'

'That's nothing to do with us,' said Thompson (which must have sounded rather aloof and unfeeling); 'What time did it happen?'

'At about 1 a.m.,' said the police officer.

'Well, why are you getting at us, then?' asked Thompson. 'At 1 a.m. we were all in a friend's house at Ashford. Why don't you ask there about us? Emery will give you the address.'

But first, the three of them must come to Brentford Police Station. So they paid their bill, and while they were doing so Thompson had the forethought to wrap his 'flick-knife' in a handkerchief and slip it over the counter to the assistant. 'Mind that for me,' he said, 'I'll be back.' Thompson later had an unexpected explanation for this, necessitated by the fact that the police at a further interview suddenly confronted him with the knife. When he wasn't out with his fruit barrow, he said, he was a tic-tac man on the racecourses, and when a tic-tac man is very busy and his pencil breaks, he has no time to fiddle about with the blades of an ordinary pocket knife. Out comes his flick-knife, a rapid piece of pencil-shapening restores business efficiency, and they're off again. 'If you'd found it on me,' said Thompson to the police officer, 'you could have said I was carrying a burgling instrument.'

(Or, he might have thought, an offensive weapon of the kind forbidden by Parliament in the Prevention of Crime Act 1953. This Act, as it happens, is of special relevance to the whole case because of the unusual resort to golf clubs as weapons of attack. If, as was widely suggested at the time, there are indeed gangs of criminals who keep sets of golf clubs in the car in order that they may be mistaken for golfers, verisimilitude demands that they do not drive about too much in the dark or crouch in the shadows when the policeman on the beat comes round. Under the Act of 1953, the most innocently-destined instrument can become the passport to two years' imprisonment unless the man in possession can show that he meant nothing but good with it.)

Once their several statements were sifted and compared, and certain other enquiries at Marlow, Watford, Ashford and Brentford were completed, they were all arrested, taken to High Wycombe, and charged. While Thompson was being finger printed and photographed, he remained (he always afterwards asserted) completely silent. And yet when they were before the Marlow magistrates a police witness said in evidence:

'While being finger printed Thompson said: "I've already told your governor we know nothing about it. We had been to Watford to do a peter." '

'What,' asked the magistrate, 'is a peter?'

' "Peter" is an underworld slang for a safe,' said the police witness.

Thompson complained strenuously, afterwards, that this allegation, which he denied, must have gravely prejudiced his case.

Now the Judges in the superior courts are always saying that if your defence amounts to a complete alibi you should disclose it at the earliest possible moment in the Magistrates' Court. Otherwise, they say, it will look as though you are keeping it up your sleeve, in order to produce it triumphantly to the jury when it is far too late for the police to make any enquiries into it. Of course, you may have said to the police, as Powers did when he was being arrested, 'We have been parked up all night,' or as Emery said, 'We've been playing cards at a pal's house all night,' or as Thompson said, 'We are in the clear, we can prove where we was.' But you do not have to prove the truth of what you say to the police, and to say it before the magistrates is much more important. Yet it is a feature of English criminal procedure that, once before the magistrates on a charge that is to be 'committed for trial' by jury, you will have no formal opportunity of doing this until the prosecution has told the whole of its story. It is true that if you have a solicitor, *and an alibi that he believes,* he will get up almost as soon as the whole thing starts and say 'Naturally, sir, we have a complete answer to all this, and the answer is simply that we weren't there.' If you have no solicitor you can shout the same thing the moment you are in court, omitting the word 'naturally'; and the clerk will say 'Yes, very well, now you be quiet until your turn comes, and then you can ask the witnesses any questions tending to show that this is a case of mistaken identity.' But it is not until the close of the proceedings, when the magistrate has decided to send you before a jury, that the formal charge is put to you and you are asked what you have to say in answer to it. (The question itself is preceded by a formal caution, so worded as to sound like a strong hint that you had far better say nothing at all.)

And whatever the judges say, the general practice in most Magistrates' Courts is for the prisoner to hold his fire, *especially if he has a criminal record.* There are two good reasons why he should do this, even where he has a genuine alibi. One is that his own solicitor probably won't believe him and will advise him to drop it; and therefore to produce the alibi too soon is to put a needless strain on solicitor-and-client relationships. The other is that when, as a long-established criminal, you find yourself wrongly accused, you often take that to be part of an unending contest in which you must 'box clever'; and it is not boxing clever to blurt out all the names and addresses of the witnesses who can prove your alibi. There may be a long interval between the magistrates' hearing and the trial by judge and jury, and during that time those witnesses of yours may retain their value the more surely for being *incognito*. An official system that can produce this tissue of false accusations against you is capable (you may genuinely believe) of getting at your witnesses if it knows who they are; and some of them are perhaps criminals enjoying a precarious liberty that the police are in a position to terminate at any moment.

Emery, Thompson and Powers, at all events, told the Marlow Magistrates that they 'pleaded Not Guilty and reserved their defence,' though their counsel had cross-examined the Crown witnesses in terms which showed that an alibi must be on the way. And upon their trial at Northampton Assizes none of them could be shaken on it.

The jury rejected it.

In his efforts to obtain legal aid after his own financial resources had failed and his solicitor had withdrawn from the case, Thompson wrote to the National Council for Civil Liberties; and the success of that organisation in getting him legal aid was the beginning of a campaign that ended in one of its most noteworthy triumphs.

After his sentence he was taken to Bedford Prison. He at once applied for leave to appeal to the Court of Criminal Appeal against his conviction. (Unless your conviction is wrong upon some point of law, you have no inherent right to appeal; and it could not be said in the case of any of these three men that the law itself, provided the alleged facts were accepted, was in error. If the conviction is challenged upon some question of fact—e.g., an alibi—then neither the Judge who tried the case nor the Court of Criminal Appeal can grant—or refuse—leave to appeal; and it was the latter consent that Thompson now sought.) It was in vain; and the Attorney-General, moreover, refused to allow him to take his case to the House of Lords. These last few kicks expended, he was taken to Stafford Prison to serve his seven year sentence.

It was at Stafford Prison, during the visits of his mother and sister, that he began to hear of the efforts being made to have his case reopened. More witnesses had been found who saw the car outside the Bloomfield's house in Desford Way, Ashford. His brother-in-law, Mr Leslie Mitchell, a part-time bookmaker, proved to be a man of extraordinary pertinacity —as did Mr Lewis Williams, Thompson's former employer. These two, fully convinced of Thompson's innocence, began a joint campaign of enquiry that took them to thirty-six prisons in England and Wales, into newspaper offices, into House of Commons committee rooms, into conferences with lawyers and (perhaps above all) to the offices of the National Council for Civil Liberties, which was co-ordinating all this activity and to which every letter and statement was carefully dispatched.

Meanwhile, a fellow prisoner at Stafford told Thompson that the men who had attacked Police Constable Pye were a 'Shepherd's Bush firm' and that he knew them. He would say no more. A little later, brought to London to defend a divorce action being brought by his wife, Thompson was lodged for the time being in Wormwood Scrubs; and on his last afternoon there he heard two other prisoners, in a discussion about a gang that carried golf clubs as weapons, refer to a case in which a policeman had been 'beaten up' and the wrong men arrested. Although he could not ascertain their names, he did learn that these golf-club gallants were now in prison themselves. Where?

An extraordinary amount of information, much of it false, permeates the prisons by way of a long established 'grapevine,' which has been doubly busy since the abolition of the 'no-talking rule' in the prisons. But Thompson was not likely to learn much through this channel in Stafford Prison, which was then almost reserved for 'star' class prisoners— men likely to have little contact with the real crime jungle. He had to wait another few months until, in May, 1955, he was transferred again to Wormwood Scrubs. It was not long then before he knew that the three men he needed to know more about were Geoffrey Joseph, William Purdy, and Frederick Robinson. (One news item that the grape-vine did not convey to him was that Emery, four months previously, had petitioned the Home Secretary naming the same three men.) Robinson, he learned, had died in prison. But Robinson's brother happened, at this moment, to be serving a sentence at Parkhurst. One morning during the Wormwood Scrubs sick parade, Thompson had a conversation with an old lag while they sat outside the Medical Officer's room awaiting their turn. This man said that he was shortly going back to Parkhurst to complete a long sentence. Thompson at once asked him if he knew Robinson's brother, who was known to his intimates as 'Yocker' Robinson; and found that he knew not only him but Geoffrey Joseph too. Thompson gave him an urgent message for these two, and then began another of those inordinate periods of waiting that in so many of the cases described in this book have spun out the process by which Justice acknowledges and redresses its own mistakes.

Meanwhile, James Powers had also heard—in the same prison, Wormwood Scrubs, but at a different time—that Joseph had confessed at Parkhurst. And Thompson's former employer, Mr Lewis Williams, of Shepherd's Bush, still busily campaigning for the re-opening of the case, one night had a cryptic telephone call at his home. 'Listen,' said an unfamiliar voice, 'are you still interested in getting young Thompson out? Right. For thirty quid I'll tell you the names of the men that hit the copper and you can pay me when the matter's all cleared up.' Mr Williams made an appointment to meet this terse informant, and was supplied with the names (plus a little of the life history and an accurate account of their respective prison addresses) of Joseph and Purdy. (Robinson, it will be remembered, had died in prison.)

It was then that Thompson, on the advice of the prison governor, sent in his petition to the Home Secretary for release. At first sight, it may seem odd that the release of a man who has been found to be serving a prison sentence for someone else's crime should be dependent on his petitioning the Home Secretary. But the confessions and admissions of prisoners have a wildly fluctuating value. A confession made before trial is very often repudiated by the man who made it, and almost as often ruled inadmissible for fear that it was made in response to some promise of favour or hope of reward. A confession made long afterwards, and in prison, may have a set of ulterior motives that are quite different without being any more altruistic. In particular, a man serving this particular kind of sentence (Purdy and Joseph were each doing fourteen years 'preventive detention,' which does not admit of any 'remission' for good conduct) has little to lose by confessing to anything short of treason or murder, even if, in prison as outside it, his confession is highly dubious; and he may have much to gain—a 'clean slate' when he comes out, a clandestine reward for his dependants during his imprisonment, an ultimate share in the proceeds of some crime more successful than his own. Or he may simply feel that he might as well do a little good to someone else by telling a pack of lies for which he cannot be punished. These considerations must be taken to account for the fact that eight long weeks elapsed before Thompson heard anything about the effect of his petition.

He was then visited by two police officers, Superintendent Lewis and Detective Sergeant Stannard, who had been detailed by Scotland Yard, at the instance of the Home Secretary, to devote their whole time to the enquiry until the matter was cleared up. In the prison interview room they took a long statement from him. 'They were kindness itself,' he said afterwards. They were also thoroughness itself. The full story of their enquiries will never be told, for it is a story that laid bare not only a succession of honest mistakes but a variety of human motives among non-police witnesses that would sustain a long series of inter-related short stories. But the enquiries occupied a busy three months and resulted in a report from Superintendent Lewis, direct to the Home Secretary, of more than three hundred pages. Typical of the many subordinate stories that had to be followed up was the history of the broken golf club. It was found to be one of a dozen that had belonged to a well-known professional golfer. When he was found, he was able to say where eleven of them had probably gone to when he sold them, and their purchasers were all traced. But the twelfth? In Parkhurst Prison, Geoffrey Joseph told Superintendent Lewis that he stole the twelfth from the shop of a London second-hand dealer; and in due course that dealer remembered the theft. In many similar ways the confessions of Joseph and Purdy were confirmed in every detail by patient enquiry.

Thus it was early November when Superintendent Lewis first visited Thompson in prison, and the latter set his hopes on being out by Christmas—until a further development raised his hopes much higher. A prisoner walking round the exercise yard at Wormwood Scrubs edged up to him and said 'Purdy's confessed.'

This was true. The two surviving assailants of Police Constable Pye had now declared, formally, that Emery, Thompson and Powers had been wrongly convicted. This was ten days before Christmas, 1955. Another month was to go by, however, before they were released from prison— on 14th January, 1956—despite their request for parole during the Christmas holiday, and despite a most unusual further development at Marlow. Mrs Saunders, wife of Police Sergeant Saunders, who was the 'officer-in-charge' at Marlow police station on that eventful night, sent a letter to the Home Secretary. 'My husband is very unhappy about the case,' she wrote, 'and thought in his own heart that the three men were not guilty as charged.' (She added, though with what authority is not known, that Police Constable Pye was also worried about his identification of the three men.) Whether or not the Sergeant approved of this letter from his wife, his position in the case may be sympathetically judged from the fact that a 'station officer's' duties in relation to the taking of charges are, in most cases, quasi-magisterial: if he thinks that the evidence in any case put before him is insufficient to justify sending it before a magistrate, he can 'refuse the charge.' This is fairly commonly done, but (unlike the dismissal of a charge by a magistrate) it necessitates a full written explanation of the decision taken; and that explanation, more often than not, is designed not merely to justify the station-officer's action but also to protect the arresting officers against possible disciplinary measures for exceeding their duty. Few people outside the police service realise the responsibility which, in this respect, rests upon the 'station officer'—who is often, and particularly in the supposedly quiet hours of the night, a quite junior sergeant 'acting' in the rank to which he next aspires. The temptation is strong, even in the face of the gravest personal doubts, to be overborne by the number or experience of others and 'let the magistrates decide.'

Two final details of identification must have caused some *post hoc* uneasiness to many of the police officers involved. First, the motor car number which was circulated to 'all ranks' on the night of the 16th October, 1953 was not known to be that of the 'Wolseley' in which Police Constable Pye's assailants drove away. It was only known to be the number of the car in which Emery, Thompson and Powers had been seen earlier in the night. Secondly, the 'Wolseley' car at Marlow High Street, it was afterwards learned, was in fact a 'Jaguar.'

The case had enlisted the attention of a number of M.P.s, and in particular the active interest of Sir Hugh Linstead and Mr W. Thomas Williams. On 24th January, 1956, Mr

Geoffrey de Freitas, a Labour Member and former Under Secretary at the Home Office, asked the Home Secretary in the House of Commons 'whether he would make a statement' on the whole case. The Home Secretary, Major Gwilym Lloyd George, retold briefly the story of the attack on Police Constable Pye before going on to say what the latest developments were. (Listening to him myself in the Strangers' Gallery, I was aware of the almost insupportable tenseness with which all large assemblies hear a statement that is of direct emotional interest to everyone present: I think you could literally have heard a pin drop, and it seemed as though we had all stopped breathing. We were looking down into the very heart of Parliament's greatest and oldest anxiety—the liberty of the subject.)

'The case against these men,' went on the Home Secretary, 'rested principally on the identification of two of them by the constable who was attacked, and of one by a civilian witness, and on the evidence of the constable and other eye witnesses as to the make or description of the car in which the men concerned drove away.

'The three men applied to the Court of Criminal Appeal for leave to appeal, but leave was refused. They petitioned maintaining their innocence. Inquiries were made into these petitions, but they adduced no new evidence and there was nothing on which I should have been justified in taking any further action. In February, 1955, Emery gave, in a petition, the names of three men who, he said, were responsible for the crime. He gave no evidence in support of this statement and there was at that time no evidence to connect the men mentioned by Emery with the crime, or to throw doubt on the evidence on which Emery, Thompson and Powers were convicted. In September, 1955, I received a petition from one of the men mentioned by Emery, who was serving a long term of preventive detention. He stated that he and another man, and a third man now dead, were responsible for the crime at Marlow.

'Confessions of this nature' (the Home Secretary continued) 'cannot be taken at their face value.' (On page 125 I venture to advance a number of reasons why this is a soundly sceptical attitude.) 'Further enquiries were, therefore, made at my request by the Buckinghamshire police, and these led me to think that the confession might be genuine. I accordingly asked the Commissioner of Police of the Metropolis to arrange for a senior officer to undertake thorough enquiries. They were carried out with the full co-operation and assistance of the Buckinghamshire police. They involved interviewing over fifty people scattered about the country, many of whom had to be seen more than once. Some of them were of bad character, and some had been in contact in prison with Emery.' (Some, as I have related, had also been in contact there with Thompson.) 'Their statements, therefore, had to be carefully checked one against the other and against the surrounding circumstances.'

This cross-checking of statements is a process, long familiar to the police, which always throws up discrepancies. Some of them, the Home Secretary thought, needed further checking; and in the course of it the more irreconcilable among them disappeared. 'I came to the conclusion,' said the Home Secretary, 'that it would be right for me to recommend the grant of "free pardons" to Emery, Thompson and Powers. . . . When a man has been imprisoned as a result of what turns out to have been a mistake, it is right that the state should make some payment as a symbol of its desire to acknowledge the error and to do what is possible to square the account between society and the individual. The payment is not an acknowledgement of liability in law. It is made *ex gratia,* and does not imply that there has been any fault or neglect on the part of the authorities. I accordingly decided that *ex gratia* payments of £300 each should be made to Emery and Powers, and £400 to Thompson. These amounts bear comparison with the few cases where people have in the past, after exercising their rights of

E

appeal, either been granted a free pardon or had their convictions quashed on a reference to the Court of Criminal Appeal' (as in the case of Oscar Slater) 'by the Secretary of State.'

And the Home Secretary sat down. The tension eased. A score of Members jumped to their feet. But it was still Mr de Freitas's question. 'Does the Home Secretary realise,' he asked, 'that whatever the circumstances of the conviction in this case, many of us feel that the sums awarded to these men were quite inadequate? . . . If the State has done wrong it should not appear to look at this matter in a niggardly fashion, as a very important principle is at stake.'

The Home Secretary said that he thought the awards were generous. It came to be regarded as one of the sayings of the year.

But a Conservative Member, Mr Rees-Davies, supported Mr de Freitas. 'In these days,' he said, 'the amounts of these damages' (though the Home Secretary had gone to some trouble to point out that they were *not* damages) 'are in no way related to the sort of sum which would be awarded at law, and I venture the submission that they *should* be so related.' He might have added a comparison between these amounts and the expenses incurred by the prisoners' friends in the campaign for their release. Mr Lewis Williams was said to have spent nearly £400 and Mr Leslie Mitchell £1,000.

There was much discussion at the time, both in and out of Parliament, as to what the three men might have been awarded by a jury in an action against the police for damages for wrongful arrest, and indeed as to whether, in view of one jury's conclusion that they were guilty, any action against the police would lie. The better view seemed to be that, as the jury in the criminal proceedings were so grievously misled on the question of personal identity, their verdict could not protect the police. But at the time this chapter was being written (January, 1957) the question was still not finally decided.

However, Mr Rees Davis raised another issue of general application to cases of wrongful conviction, which still remains to puzzle the ordinary logical citizen. 'In the light of the evidence,' he said, 'is it clear that that evidence, in the circumstances, did not amount to perjury? If it did, is consideration being given to appropriate action?'

In other words, hadn't the police been lying, and the witnesses who looked from their bedroom windows in Marlow High Street, and the others who so clearly saw what kind of car it was? And were all these now to be prosecuted for perjury?

'The only perjury that occurred,' said the Home Secretary, 'or which has come to light as the result of the enquiry, was that of the prisoners themselves. Indeed, I have it on the authority of the trial Judge to say that had they not perjured themselves so much during the course of the trial they probably would not have been convicted. . . . It must be remembered that one alibi at least of one of the prisoners was that they were not concerned in the attack on the policeman, because they were in fact on the way to steal a safe in Watford.'

(It will be remembered that it was Thompson who was alleged by the police to have remarked, while they were taking his finger prints, that 'we had been to Watford to do a peter.' He made a considerable point, both at the trial and after his release, of denying that he had ever said it.)

It was all very well, concluded the Home Secretary, for M.P.s to complain that the police had been 'unable at the start to verify what obviously everybody now knows to be the truth.' Had it not been for the confessions of the two men doing preventive detention, no one would have known what the truth was. He did not remind the House that the names of those two men were supplied to him by Emery in February

1955, and that nothing was done about this until, *six months later,* one of them (perhaps tired of waiting to be asked?) wrote to the Home Office and confessed. That confession, he said, had then to be confirmed. 'It was a confirmation of the confession, after a very brilliant piece of work by the police themselves, greatly assisted by the Buckinghamshire police, which made it possible for me to take the action which I was very glad to take. . . . If the men had not stuck to their story at the trial, which the Judge said was palpably false and which the jury said was false, they might well not have been convicted.'

But they still stuck to it, even after release; and it is not difficult for anyone with a little knowledge of criminals to give it some credence. The way they spent that night was a way in which their kind do spend frequent nights, often—but not inevitably—boding no good for somebody; though as an exposition of reasons why they could not have attacked the policeman at Marlow, their story, properly supported, should have been at least as effective as if they had been in prison all the time.

There remained two unresolved mysteries. First, as Mr Emanuel Shinwell asked the Home Secretary, 'if these men are now regarded as innocent of the crimes alleged against them . . . why is it necessary to use the term "free pardon"? Of what have they been pardoned if they have not committed any crime? Ought they not to be conceded an apology for what has occurred?'

The expression had been used over many years, said the Home Secretary—'I have known people query it on one or two occasions.' (This was a modest statement: nearly every case of 'pardoning' an innocent man is followed by bewildered letters to the newspapers, often culminating in leading articles for the abolition of 'this pompous and stupid denial of justice.') But 'I am quite prepared to look at the matter,' said the Home Secretary.

By the following week he seemed to have looked at it. 'It has the sanction of long usage,' he said again, 'and it would be difficult to find another form of words which would be appropriate in the various circumstances in which the grant of a free pardon may be recommended. The document in which Her Majesty signifies her pleasure is so worded as to avoid the implication that the pardon is of an offence. It states that the pardon is of conviction and remits its legal consequences. Pardon in this sense does not mean forgiveness, but the remission of the penal consequences of a conviction.'

This is historically true. Pardons from the Crown are 'free' or 'conditional.' A conditional one may, in a capital case, involve going to prison for 'life' as an alternative to being executed, though this is more commonly, today, called a reprieve. A 'free' pardon is granted to persons whose degree of culpability may vary widely, from the motorist whose conviction under the Road Traffic Act is invalid because a 'Halt' sign was not properly placed, to the confessed burglar who 'turns Queen's evidence' against his pals to save his own skin. Sir John Fielding used to maintain that 'free pardons' of the latter kind ought to entail transportation for life: criminals, he said, would then be even more ready to impeach their accomplices, because it was so much nicer for them abroad than in this country. So there hangs, inevitably, about the word 'pardon' an aura of excused delinquency that must be galling to the wrongly convicted person, and it cannot even be said, in defence of any Parliamentary speciousness, that the legal meaning of the word itself has changed.

A wrongful conviction should be quashed, formally and in open Court—and, in such cases as that of Emery, Thompson and Powers—quashed in the Court of Criminal Appeal. The Home Secretary has power, under section 19 of the Criminal Appeal Act, 1907, to remit such cases to that Court for rehearing. The case should be given absolute priority in the

Court lists; and the appellants (already known, be it remembered, to be innocent) should meanwhile be released on parole. On 26th January, 1956, the Home Secretary was asked by Mr Ben Parkin, M.P. why he didn't allow bail to 'prisoners the validity of whose conviction is being officially investigated or reviewed.' This was too easy. 'I've no power to release convicted prisoners on bail,' said the Home Secretary. 'The question, therefore, does not arise.' Parliament should give him the power; not to 'release on bail' (since there might well be cases in which the wronged man had neither property nor friends) but to release on parole, without financial undertaking. Emery, Thompson and Powers were in prison for weeks after their innocence was conclusively established.

Secondly, a peculiarly poignant aspect of the values of personal identity: throughout all the perfectly justified indignation over the Government's niggardly award to these three men, which at least looked as though someone at the top had said 'Oh, give the scamps a thousand between them,' no one expressed any concern about compensation for the injured policeman. P.C. Pye had had a long illness after the attack in which he had been so severely injured. Let us grant at once that he got full pay while he was on sick leave, plus medical attention and convalescence. Is it popularly supposed that he got anything else? A man suffering such injuries at the hands of another who was rich enough to pay appropriate damages might well recover £5,000 on the verdict of a compassionate jury. Emery, Thompson and Powers, though they only got £1000 between them, may well have been of less aggregate value to the community than was P.C. Pye on his own; and the latter was at least doing his dangerous duty—Mr Justice Stable congratulated him, at Northamptonshire Assizes, on 'his very great courage and presence of mind in extremely adverse conditions.' Bearing in mind what the lawyers would call 'pain and suffering,' to say nothing of a changed social life and the expense and

inconvenience to his family of visiting him in hospital, why
not some kind of payment, even *ex gratia*, to the policeman?
But we may have to wait a long time before even the Welfare
State will show the same concern for victims of criminal
assault (night watchmen, bank messengers, policemen, as
well as women and girls) as it does for people injured in
industrial accidents, or even for persons of bad character
who get convicted for crimes they have not done.

The vindication of Emery, Thompson and Powers was
justly described by the National Council for Civil Liberties,
in their Annual Report for 1955–6, as 'an achievement of the
year.' Not only had a wrong been righted, said the Report:
'attention has been drawn to many weaknesses in our legal
system, and we are glad to have had a share in this action.'
The Council was modest in calling it a share. It first learned
of the case when Thompson wrote to it for help in getting
legal aid, a development that should never be necessary if
the terms of the Legal Aid and Advice Act, 1949, were
faithfully observed by the magistrates. The Council heard
no more until after the men were sentenced, and of course
had no sound reason then to believe that they were innocent
of the charge against them. When the men's appeals had
been rejected by the Court of Criminal Appeal, the Council
further examined the case at the instance of Thompson's
relatives. From a study of the depositions and the transcript
of the Judge's summing up, the following points emerged:

(1)   The identification took place without any identifica-
      tion parade. The injured police officer made the
      identification from photographs brought to him by
      a senior officer. (Perhaps I may interject here that
      identification by photographs, though perfectly law-
      ful, goes far to invalidate any subsequent 'parade,'
      but also conveys to the court that the accused person
      has been photographed by the police on the occasion
      of some previous conviction.)

(2) The identification by the woman who saw the attack from the window seems similarly to have been made from photographs. Moreover, her husband, who was with her, was unable to identify anyone, and her own evidence in the Magistrates' Court was that the attacker (who, be it remembered, was wearing a nylon stocking over his head and face) was 'like Emery';

(3) A further witness who gave a somewhat different account of the happenings was not called at the trial;

(4) No reference was made by the prosecution to finger prints on any of the weapons used. No implements were found on any of the three men when they were seen by the police at the café;

(5) Despite the amount of blood spilt, no bloodstains were found on either of the men alleged to have made the assault. (But Superintendent Lewis found bloodstains in the Jaguar car when he examined it two years later!)

(6) Despite the fact that neither the injured policeman nor any of the witnesses had the number of the car involved, the police warning which went out immediately after the incident gave the number of the car the three men were using. It appears that this car had been noted by the police earlier in the evening in connection with another matter. (As I have explained, a Scotland Yard message to Bucks police had said that Emery, Thompson and Powers were on their way to commit a crime with it.)

The Council for Civil Liberties thought that although these six points were 'disquieting,' they would not by themselves be enough to upset the convictions. It was eventually decided to open independent investigations. With Mr Lewis Williams and Mr Leslie Mitchell, respectively the former

employer and the brother-in-law of Thompson, a member
of the Council's legal panel made exhaustive enquiries in
the Ashford district, and took statements from a number
of further witnesses who testified to the presence of the
three men or of their car at Ashford at the crucial time.
Sir Hugh Linstead, Thompson's M.P., asked the Council to
send its memorandum and other relevant documents to the
Home Secretary; and only then did the official enquiry
begin.

Among the Council's final recommendations were the
following, which, I have found, command wide assent among
lawyers, and which would undoubtedly reduce the risk of
mistaken identity in criminal cases.

(1)   There should be a complete review of methods used
       for identifying suspects, with particular reference to
       the use of photographs. (The Home Office have
       many times rejected this proposal. Suggestions that
       may be worth considering are put forward in Chapter
       III (Identification Parades)).

(2)   Transcripts of trials should be made available not
       only to convicted persons desirous of appealing but
       also, at a proper charge, to convicted persons who
       don't necessarily want to appeal and to any other
       persons desirous of obtaining them. (At present they
       are obtainable only by 'an interested party,' and the
       phrase is so interpreted by the Court of Criminal
       Appeal as to rule out, in many cases, persons
       acting on behalf of a prisoner. I personally should
       not contend that they ought literally to be avail-
       able to anyone, regardless of motive for wanting
       them.)

(3)   In cases where a conviction is, in effect, quashed by
       the Home Secretary, the word 'pardon' should not
       be used. A more suitable term should be found. (I
       would suggest, in cases where the conviction is wrong

on the facts, as distinct from an invalidating legal
or procedural error, the use of the word 'exoner-
ation.')

(4) Compensation for imprisonment, where the conviction is shown to be wrongful (and, I should again
add, where it is wrong *on the facts*), should be given
as of right; and a committee should be established
to determine the amounts. These should, in all cases,
cover out-of-pocket expenses and a minimum for
general compensation.

As I implied at the beginning of this chapter, the case of
Emery, Thompson and Powers occurred at a time when both
the House of Commons and the general public were
in some measure prepared for a limitation in the use of the
death penalty for murder. Whatever might happen in the
future, it was plain that the murder of a policeman would not
be generally regarded as a crime to be dealt with in any other
way than by death. For some time it must have seemed
likely that the injured policeman might die. If his death had
occurred 'within a year and a day' from the hour of half-past
one on the morning of 16th October, 1953, the law would
have regarded him as a murdered man and his assailants
as eligible to suffer death by hanging. 'The law of England,'
said Sir James FitzJames Stephen in his *History of the
Criminal Law of England*, 'has laid down an arbitrary rule
for criminal purposes upon this subject.' (i.e. the time-lapse
between the deed and the death). 'No one would say, for
instance, that a man's parents had caused his death by
causing his birth. The only cases worth examining are those
which illustrate the limit. One obvious limit is length of
time. Instances of death from wounds or other injuries
received many years before death are not unknown. In some
cases of this sort the connection is clear. In general it would
be obscure . . . No one is criminally responsible for a death
which occurs upwards of a year and a day (that is, more than

a complete year reckoning the whole of the last day of the year) after the act by which it was caused.'

In statements made to the Press after their release from prison, Emery, Thompson and Powers showed plainly enough that they had been well aware that their lives were in jeopardy during the first year of their imprisonment. There would, however, have been a complete retrial, on a fresh indictment for murder; and the lessons of the first trial would perhaps have been sufficient to eliminate some of the errors, both of commission and omission, that had vitiated its result. Nevertheless, there must be a special quality about the fear of hanging when you are inside a prison and cannot even give the police a run for their money. For this reason perhaps above all, no more disturbing case of mistaken identity has occurred in this century.

In his recent book, *Portraits from Memory,** Bertrand Russell can suggest only one possible remedy for the growing danger to individual liberties in the modern State; 'and that,' he says, 'is the establishment of a second police force designed to prove innocence, not guilt.' Noting the popular belief that it is better to let ninety-nine guilty men escape than to punish one innocent man, he says: 'Our institutions are founded upon the opposite view. If a man is accused, for example, of a murder, all the resources of the State, in the shape of policemen and detectives, are employed to prove his guilt, whereas it is left to his individual efforts to prove his innocence ... A police force designed to prove innocence should never attempt to prove guilt except in one kind of case: namely, where it is the authorities who are suspected of crime. I think' (adds Bertrand Russell) 'that the creation of such a police force might enable us to preserve some of our traditional liberties, but I do not think that any lesser measure will do so.'

It is often overlooked that a police enquiry, in finding proof that someone committed a crime, is thus finding proof

* Allen & Unwin, 1956.

that a number of other suspects did not. In the case of Emery, Thompson and Powers, one police enquiry proved their guilt of a crime of which they knew nothing, and a second one, which took much longer, proved their innocence. Perhaps the second one showed that if Bertrand Russell's proposal is ever taken up, we can use the same police force to do the two jobs, possibly on alternate days.

IX

THE
SPLIT PERSONALITY

A FEW years ago an Old Bailey Judge was confronted, as
Judges increasingly are, with evidence that the man
he was about to sentence was schizophrenic.

'In fact, if I accept this evidence at its face value,' he said
to the prisoner, 'You are really two men, and only one of
you is really guilty of this offence. Well, I'm afraid both of
you must go to prison.'

It takes less than this to make a court laugh. The court
laughed. Many people still think that schizophrenia is
modern medico-psychological jargon for Jekyll and Hyde.
But schizophrenia is certainly an aspect of the relationship
between individual and group. And the development of the
multiple personality demanded of even the most ordinary
person by modern social conditions is so interesting a process
that I propose to digress here and examine it.

You have to imagine, for this purpose, a man cast away
on an uninhabited island without hope of rescue. He has
been there twenty years, free from all the restraints that
ordinarily impose or require the simplest concessions to
decency and toleration, when a second castaway arrives,
similarly bereft of any hope of rescue. They meet. You
have to suppose that the question whether they shall fight
to the death or work out a *modus vivendi* is resolved
in favour of keeping alive, and they begin their life
together.

Now, whereas there was at first on the island only one

personality, only one identity, there are now—two? No: four. There is the one that each of them knows (or believes) to be his true self, and the one that he presents (or believes himself to present) to the other. If ever they are rescued and return to the communal life of a modern State, they must begin then to present further personalities to their daily contacts among the citizens, some developed on lines that lead in oddly contrasting directions. If in the course of an average year you meet, on speaking terms, a thousand people whose paths cross your own repeatedly, you could conceivably show them a thousand differing identities— and find, in the process, that the essential self gets more and more difficult to isolate. The fact that each of those thousand people is also meeting his thousand others involves mathematical complexities that I have always lacked the courage to follow. I return to the isolation and recognition of the self.

This, I believe, is where the psychologist can help, whether or not he is a doctor—or a priest. And it is among the defeated, the failures in this complicated game, that the psychiatrist finds many of the people who, he tells us, suffer from that large class of mental illnesses that are lumped together as schizophrenia—Jung's state of being 'a dreamer in a world awake.' It can hardly have occurred to Dr Eugen Bleuler, who suggested the word schizophrenia in 1911 as a group name for all these mental illnesses (till then called dementia præcox), that his word would pass into ordinary speech within two decades; but it was he who first showed that those illnesses of the mind had, as their outstanding characteristic, 'a partial breakdown of the normal associative bonds and integrity of the entire personality.' Dr David Stafford-Clark describes schizophrenia as 'a disintegration of thought, emotion, and behaviour,' and thinks that what lies at the root of the disease is 'a withdrawal of interest from external reality, and the surrender of a feeling of responsibility for conforming to its demands.' This withdrawal, he says, occurs because the stresses of living threaten the personality with unbearable emotions, 'imperfectly assimilated and hitherto repressed;' and the effect of it is

> not simply to remove the patient's mental life from the same basis of participation in reality as that shared by others, but, at the price of admittedly terrible illness, to render unnecessary on the one hand further repression, or, on the other, any attempt at conscious control of such treacherous mechanisms as projection and displacement.*

The afflicted person is said, at such times, to be going through a 'schizophrenic episode.'

Miles Giffard, the 26-year-old son of a former Under-Sheriff of Cornwall, was said by two experienced psychiatrists to be schizophrenic. His pointless, motiveless, and unconcealed murder of his father and mother in the summer of 1952 is best described in the words of his own statements to the police and to his solicitors. The story may be thought to illustrate the almost minute-by-minute changes that occur, in the case of a schizophrenic, in the relationship of the ego to the rest of that personality which, as I have said, he tries to present to the external world; and it may be borne in mind, as one reads the story, that this was a young man who had been an inordinately sensitive and intractable child, who had received psychiatric treatment for two and half years as a boy at a public school, and whose adolescence and early manhood were marked by social inadequacy, dishonesty, untidiness, and general shiftlessness.

'I want to be frank,' he said at Scotland Yard. 'I did it . . . I want to tell you the whole story. Many of the things I have said' (in an earlier statement) 'are not true. I haven't been working for about twelve months. I have only said these things to make a bold front to her' (his fiancée).

* *Psychiatry Today*. Penguin Books. 1952.

'Up to about twelve months ago I was studying; firstly for the law, as a solicitor, and latterly as an estate agent. My father made me an allowance of £5 a month. I couldn't settle down to my studies, and this led to some differences between me and my father. I gave up working last November' (1951), 'and then I got a legacy of £750. I had spent the money by about March. I scrounged around a bit and did some work—about eight weeks. I was selling ice-cream for Walls. I left them, and some time in June' (1952) 'I went home and broke into my father's house' (at Carrickowl, near St Austell.) 'Then I came to London and spent the money. I was only in London for a week, staying at odd hotels, and then I went down to my home again. Then I returned to London to dispose of some of the stuff I had taken—a cine-camera, and a bracelet of my mother's. I sold the camera at a place called Photo-Optics at Paddington. I sold the bracelet with Dawson, the jeweller at Piccadilly Circus. Then I went home (I was only up here for a day). I straightened it out with my father.' (That completely amoral 'straightened it out' is worth keeping in mind.)

'I stayed home until the middle of August, and then I came to London. I lived in Chelsea and took a furnished room. I began to visit the White Hart public house in King's Road, Chelsea. I met a Chelsea pensioner who frequented that public house. About a month ago—no, six weeks ago— he introduced me to a young lady and her mother, with whom I became great friends.* I became a frequent visitor at their house, where I was made very welcome.

'I had been living from hand to mouth. I had odd bits of money from various people, and there are some cheques which were "R.D." I'd been drinking very heavily, and about a month ago the girl began charging me about my untidy appearance. I told her my parents had arranged to

---

* He named a girl of about nineteen and her mother, and gave their address. They were of course entirely respectable people, whose name is in no way necessary to this story.

send my clothing up, but this was a lie just to stall her off. I was tight for money at this time and had no means of tidying myself up; so about a fortnight ago I said I would go home and get my clothing myself. That is what I told her, but in fact I wanted to go home to try and get some money from my father. On Friday, 31st October, 1952, I decided to hitch-hike home and I told her so. She was rather upset at my going.

'I went, arriving on 2nd November. (I actually did hitch-hike.) I phoned her practically every day. I had a row with my father over my spending habits, and told her so; he had said I was to stop at home and continue with my studies. She suggested that I should come up to London, get a job, and make myself independent of my parents. I decided to come back to London the following week-end— that is this week-end . . . I telephoned her twice on the Friday, 7th November, the first time at half-past five. I told her I was coming up to do some business for my father. This wasn't true. I promised to phone her again at half-past eight to confirm whether in fact I was coming; and I told her if I did come my father had promised to let me use his car—it is a Triumph, the number is ERL 1.

'At the time of my first call my father and mother were both out. They came back almost together in separate cars at about 7.30 p.m. My father was doing something to my mother's car. Both cars were in the garage. God knows for what reason, I hit them over the head with a piece of iron pipe. I hit him first, and he slumped to the ground un-conscious. Mother had gone into the house. I went into the house after her. I found her in the kitchen; I hit her from behind. Everything went peculiar—I got into a panic.

'Shortly after this I made a second phone call to the girl in London—this was about 8.15—and told her I was definitely coming to London with my father's car. I asked

if I could come round to her house in the morning for a
wash and shave.'

It is interesting to observe that at the moment when he was
having this mildly domestic conversation with a girl-friend
in London, both his parents lay dying from head wounds
he had inflicted on them a few moments before. Later, when
he wrote reassuringly to the girl from prison—which he did
daily for seventy-eight days—he said: 'Anything can
happen . . . I think you should go out and see people. After
all, if everything is all right we can still take up where we
left off.'

His statement to the police continued: 'I went out with
the intention of getting the car and found my father coming
round. I hit him again, several times. Then I got the car
out, and went in to get some clothes. My mother was coming
round, then. So I hit *her* again. She was bleeding very
heavily: they both were by this time. I didn't know what
to do; there was blood everywhere. I got the wheelbarrow,
put my mother in it, took her out to the Point' (i.e. a nearby
cliff-edge at Porthpean) 'and pushed her over. I then went
back and did the same with my father's body. I pushed
the wheelbarrow over, that time. Then I went back to the
house and washed the place out. I went to my mother's
room and took some pieces of jewellery. (The two brooches
and the ring shown to me are some of the jewellery.)
And I took some money from my father's coat pocket.
I packed a change of clothing; my own clothes were very
bloodstained.

I then drove the car out and drove to London. I changed
my clothing before I got to Okehampton—I threw the pair
of flannel trousers and tweed sports coat, which were very
blood-stained, into a river at Fenny Bridges, just past Exeter.
I also threw the piece of steel tubing I had hit my mother
and father with into the river at the same time. I then drove

on to London. I picked up two hitch-hikers somewhere near Ilchester—I dropped them at Chelsea Bridge. I then went on to . . . Street' (where his girl friend lived in Chelsea), got there about 5 a.m., and parked the car in the side of the road about fifty or sixty yards from the house. I had a sleep in the car until about eight o'clock. Then I left the car and went to the house, where I saw her and her mother. When I left the car I left the ignition key in it, and also left some blood-stained clothing in it, and shoes. This blood came on to my clothes when I moved my mother and father.'

(One should note, here, not only that this residue of his blood-stained clothing was still in the car, with some blood-stained letters and paper money, but that he was still going about—and continued to do so till the moment of his arrest —wearing a shirt with deeply blood-dyed cuffs and sleeves and a tie that was unmistakably bloodstained. Moreover, he had given a lift to two strangers on the Exeter-London Road, and had driven straight to the address where the police would first seek him. Yet the prosecution, at his trial, sought to show that he had consistently tried to cover up all traces of his crime.)

'I told her,' he went on, referring to the girl, 'I was up to do some business for my father and that I had put the car in the Blue Star Garage. I said I had an appointment at ten o'clock and that I would come back to lunch. I went off to Dawson's, at Piccadilly Circus, where I sold three pieces of my mother's jewellery for £50. Later I telephoned the girl and told her I couldn't keep the luncheon appointment, and that I would meet her at 2 p.m. at Leicester Square. I later met her and her mother—at two o'clock. We went to the Odeon Cinema, Leicester Square, and saw *Limelight*. We left there at five o'clock and I went off on my own with the girl. We went to a public house and had a meal, then we made a round of various public houses, eventually arriving at the Star, Chesham Mews, where, upon leaving, I told her what I had done, that I had murdered my father and mother.'

(As if it had just come back into his mind. A little shopping in the morning, the sale of some trinkets, an afternoon watching Charlie Chaplin, an evening meal and a 'round of the public houses,' and then: 'I've murdered my father and mother!')

'It upset her very much,' the statement went on, 'and we just moved to further public houses drinking. I told her that she would not be seeing me again. I had previously booked a room at the Regent Palace Hotel in the name of Gregory. I think I told her that I was staying with relatives in St John's Wood.

'Later I took a taxi—after closing time—and took her back to her home. I was very drunk, and after she had left the cab, and I was being driven away, I remember it being stopped.'

It was stopped by the police, who at that time were ostensibly looking for the driver of the 'stolen' car, ERL.1; and he was arrested.

'I had some sleeping pills which I had taken from my mother's bedroom; they were in my coat pocket. I intended to take them and kill myself. That's the whole truthful story. I can only say I have had a brain storm. I can't account for my actions. I'd drunk about half a bottle of whisky on the Friday afternoon before all this happened. It just seemed to me that nothing mattered as long as I got back to London. The girl just fascinated me.'

At the trial at Bodmin Assizes, in February, 1953, before Mr Justice Oliver, a plea of 'not guilty' was entered on Giffard's behalf and the defence was that of insanity. Although, therefore, the facts were not in dispute, the whole story had to be gone through again, and all the witnesses examined and cross-examined; because while the defence relied on the incredible story itself, at least in part, to prove that its leading character was insane, the prosecution relied on the same story to prove that he was not.

At this point one should consider the relevant passage in the 'rules' by which the Judges consider themselves bound in directing juries on the question of insanity as an excuse for crime—any crime, however grave or trivial. They are known as the M'Naghten Rules (a century ago they were called 'The Rules in M'Naghten's Case') because they arose out of an attempted murder by an allegedly mentally-defective man named Daniel M'Naghten in 1843; and they were laid down by the Judges of the Queen's Bench Division, after a prolonged dispute, on one of the rare occasions when they have consented to answer a specific questionnaire, on a matter of general principle, put to them out of court. Here are the relevant words:

> 'The jury ought to be told in all cases that every man is presumed to be sane, and to possess a sufficient degree of reason to be responsible for his crimes, until the contrary be proved to their satisfaction; and that, to establish a defence on the grounds of insanity, it must be clearly proved that, at the time of the committing of the act, the party accused was labouring under such a defect of reason, from disease of the mind, as not to know the nature and quality of the act he was doing, or, if he did know it, that he did not know he was doing what was wrong.'

This pronunciamento, which contrives to be at once vague and arbitrary, has probably sustained more legal argument than any other accepted principle of the criminal law of England, though in the United States and some of the Dominions it is now falling into disrepute. The sanity of a prisoner is a 'rebuttable presumption'; and to rebut it, his defenders must prove that when he committed the act his mind was so diseased that he could not know the 'nature and quality' of it.

What did the Judges mean by 'nature and quality?' Two different attributes of the same act? No, said the Court of Criminal Appeal in *R. v. Codere* (1916); certainly these two words have sometimes been taken to refer to a distinction between the physical character and the legal aspect of the act done, but this is wrong. 'They apply alone to the physical character, and were not intended to draw a distinction between the physical and moral aspects of the act.' In other words, they are verbiage. 'The nature and quality of the act he was doing' means 'what he was doing.'

Must he be shown to have known that it was against the criminal law, or merely that it was morally or ethically wrong? The M'Naghten Rules have something to say on this, too:

> 'If the question were to be put as to the knowledge of the accused, solely and exclusively with reference to the law of the land, it might tend to confound the jury, by inducing them to believe that an actual knowledge of the law of the land was essential in order to lead to a conviction, whereas the law is administered upon the principle that everyone must be taken conclusively to know it without proof that he does know it. If the accused was conscious that the act was one which he ought not to do, and if that act was at the same time contrary to the law of the land, he is punishable; and the usual course, therefore, has been to leave the question to the jury, whether the party accused had a sufficient degree of reason to know that he was doing an act that was wrong. This course, we think, is correct.'

'An act that was wrong?' You will notice, in the extract just quoted, that the Rules hold a man punishable if he 'was conscious that the act done was *one which he ought not to do*.' And the 'ought not' was to be found in something other than the law of the land, because that was brought in as a separate source of morality. Yet in 1952 the Court of

Criminal Appeal decided that the word 'wrong' here means 'contrary to the law,' and 'does not have a further meaning of morally wrong'; the court seems to have been forced into this rejection of the M'Naghten wrongness by the need to decide (in *R. v. Windle*, 36 Cr.App. R.85) that

> in these Rules the word 'wrong' means contrary to the law, and does not have a further meaning of morally wrong, and that it would not be a defence to prove that although the prisoner knew a particular act to be against the law, he believed that in his own view, or in the view of a number of persons, large or small, the act might be justified.

It was in this curious state of the law as to insanity and intention that Mr Justice Oliver and the jury, in the case of Miles Giffard, heard the evidence of three doctors, two of whom said that the prisoner suffered from schizophrenia and was insane at the time when he killed his parents, while the other said that he would have known what he was doing and that it was 'wrong.' There was evidence that, as a young child, he had been nervous and always exceptionally small for his age, that between the age of two and four he was in the care of a nurse who beat him and locked him in dark cupboards, and that the family doctor, called in because of his nervous condition, advised the dismissal of the nurse. The nurse was not dismissed. When at last she left of her own accord, she was succeeded by an affectionate sixteen-year-old girl to whom he became very attached and who stayed five years with him. She gave evidence about his frequent screaming nightmares and the great difficulty of bringing him back to consciousness and reality. At the age of fifteen he was taken to a psychiatrist—who thought at first that he was twelve—and he attended for treatment several times weekly for two years.

Among the items of evidence offered by the prosecution, presumably directed to the question of Giffard's sanity, was the opinion of the pathologist that the blows that killed the two victims, although heavy, 'had not been struck with maniacal frenzy.'

A letter he wrote to the girl in Chelsea is as revealing as any other circumstance as to the state of responsibility in which he moved and behaved shortly before the murder:

What I was afraid would happen has happened. I have had the hell of a row with the old man—made far worse by the fact that, as usual, he is right. Anyway, the upshot of the whole thing is that he has forbidden me to return to London, at any rate for the time being. He says he will cut me off without even the proverbial shilling, so there does not seem to be any alternative until I can get a job. You seem fated to miss my beautiful clothes . . .

I am dreadfully fed up and miserable, as I was especially looking forward to seeing you tomorrow; and God and the old man (hereinafter called the O.M.) know when I shall. Short of doing him in, I see no future in the world at all. He has stopped my allowance anyway, is giving me a pint of beer and 20 cigs a day, and has said 'no pubs.' No doubt your mother would approve. Give her my love and tell her when she next sees me I shall be a reformed character (nominally anyway).

My sweet, I love you terribly and it really is breaking my heart to leave you in that den of wolves there. God bless you and write to me soon and often. All my love, my precious. Yours, Miles.

Four days later this curious creature, who was later to be held fully responsible in law, who 'saw no future in the world' unless he killed his father but has given no hint of what future he saw if he did, killed both his parents because he wanted to go and see his girl. Besides, he needed a car.

'He may have been a bad lot, a scamp,' said Mr John Maude, Q.C., in his speech to the jury for the defence, 'but never previously, even when intoxicated, had he shown any signs of violence. Does it seem likely, therefore, that when he killed his parents he was in his sane mind? It was nothing short of absolutely crazy that he should kill them in order to drive to London to see a girl friend. He was motoring himself straight to the gallows. There was no hope in it whatsoever. Having battered his parents to death, he put them over a cliff in a wheelbarrow and then drove off to London, picking up two hitch-hikers. Are those the actions of a sane man? I ask you, members of the jury, to say that when Giffard killed his father and mother he did not know that what he was doing was unlawful. I submit to you that the overall picture is a mad one.'

Mr Scott Henderson, Q.C., spoke for the Crown. 'This case,' he said, 'is not one of a man behaving normally up to a certain point, when suddenly he goes wrong and commits a heinous crime. It is one of a man who has lived an idle and dissolute life since 1947, going from bad to worse. It is not suggested that he is insane now. The question is whether he was insane on the day of the murder. Three eminent psychiatrists have been called, and there is a complete conflict of evidence as to whether he has a mental disease. Unless you are satisfied, members of the jury, that at the time of the killing Giffard was not responsible at law because of insanity, you must return a verdict of guilty.'

It was now for Mr Justice Oliver to sum up. 'I must emphasise,' he said, 'that the only question you have to decide is whether Giffard knew when he killed his father that his act was contrary to the law.' (In this, the Judge was following, as he must, the decision in *R. v. Windle*—see page 151) 'In that matter, the burden is not on the prosecution—it is on the defence. Unfortunately, there is no gauge of human wickedness outside the law . . . It has been said that the presence of a policeman would probably not have deterred him from killing. I cannot help wondering whether the presence of a policeman might not have prevented this man going to his mother's bedroom, after he had thrown her over the cliff, and taking her jewellery. Why should a man who doesn't know that he has done wrong want to wash the blood off, throw away his weapon, change his clothes? Those actions might seem to the jury to point strongly in the direction that he knew what he had done, and that what he had done was wrong.' (Again, the Judge must have meant 'contrary to the law,' even if Giffard, through some schizophrenic or other mental confusion, did not know that it was contrary to morality.) 'After reaching London,' his Lordship went on, 'he sold his mother's jewellery for £50. Is that the act of a madman? Or is that the act of an utterly wicked man? . . . He could have gone into the witness box perfectly well, and been asked to answer some of the questions which might seem to you to be unanswerable. At least we could have asked him why he threw his mother into the sea and his father over the cliff. He might have thrown some light on it, but he has not been given the chance. His memory is perfect. He knows everything that happened, and everything he did, and all the order in which he did it. Why should he not come and tell us?'

Let us pause at that stage of Mr Justice Oliver's summing-up to reflect that Giffard's whole recollection of the story has one outstanding quality of what is called a 'schizophrenic episode': it is entirely visual and dynamic, like the recollection of a dream—it does not report words or conversations. Yet his apparently clear picture of what had happened was, through the trial and now in the summing-up, suggested as a principal ground for holding him consciously responsible for it. If he was indeed, in Jung's phrase, 'a dreamer in a world awake,' he seemed to a Judge and jury too much awake to earn the somnambulist's immunity from blame.

'There is no question,' concluded the Judge, 'but that Giffard killed his father' (the actual indictment only charged the murder of the father, the one relating to the mother being 'left on the file.') 'The sole thing disputed is whether the evidence has made it more likely than not that in your view, at the time he did it, he suffered from a disease of the mind whereby he was not able to know that what he was doing was contrary to the law.'

The jury found him guilty after only half an hour, and he was sentenced to death. A week later, a woman juror wrote to the Home Secretary, Sir David Maxwell-Fyfe, to say that at the trial she was convinced that Miles Giffard was insane when he killed his parents. There has been no public disclosure as to what had actually happened in the jury room, but the juror's letter, a copy of which was sent to Giffard's solicitors, said that because of a misunderstanding the dissentient opinion had not been made known to the Judge when the jury had returned into court. What happened was what almost always happens:

'Members of the jury, are you agreed upon your verdict?'

'We are.'

'Do you find the prisoner at the bar, Miles William Giffard, guilty or not guilty upon this indictment?'

'Guilty.'

'You find the prisoner guilty, and that is the verdict of you all?'

And the foreman replied: 'Yes, that is the verdict of us all.'

No member of the jury raised a dissentient voice in court, and the pronouncement of sentence was uninterrupted.

Whether or not any petition for the reprieve of a convicted murderer is submitted to the Home Secretary, every case is examined by him—or, to be exact, by his permanent staff—

for possible reasons, within the law and the scope of the Royal prerogative of mercy, why the execution should not be carried out. If there is a petition, it is one of the many matters thus considered. If there has been any question of insanity in any form, whether or not the M'Naghten Rules could have been stretched to include it, the prisoner is seen by a panel of three doctors approved by the Home Secretary —whose decision is not fettered by any Judge-made rules. Miles Giffard and his solicitors decided not to go to the Court of Criminal Appeal, which could not in any event— such is its peculiar and, in my view, crippled constitution— have considered the juror's disclosure because it was a matter arising after the trial. Instead the juror's letter was made the basis of a direct appeal to the Home Secretary for a reprieve, and it was accompanied by the report of a well-known psychiatrist who examined Giffard while he was awaiting execution and concluded that he was probably insane at the time of the murders, and by a long report from the Bishop of Coventry, who had been the headmaster of Giffard's school during the mental illnesses of his boyhood.

Giffard was hanged at 9 a.m. on 24 February 1953.

For the limited purposes of this book, the case of Miles Giffard illustrates how the human personality, as an integration of disparate selves, is regarded by the law. The relationship is between 'ego-control,' consciousness, and the awareness of social obligation. Does a schizophrenic know, when he breaks the law, 'the nature and quality of the act he is doing,' and if he does know it, does he 'know he is doing what is wrong?' If so, who is it that does the act and knows it to be wrong? It is perhaps wise to admit that mental patients, especially violent or socially dangerous ones, are sometimes amenable to punishment; and it is a logically held view that you may well retard the recovery of a mental patient who is under treatment if you deprive him of the exercise supplied by punishment, or the prospect of it, to the growing moral consciousness. But when you kill a schizophrenic patient because he has done wrong, and because the M'Naghten Rules pre-date Freud and Bleuler by fifty years, do you know 'the nature and quality of the act' that you are doing?

'I'm afraid that both of you must go to prison.'

X

THE
DRUCE-PORTLAND CASE

I REMEMBER that it was only after some years of rather
desultory religious instruction, of the kind that was then
thought consonant with the aims of the Education Acts,
that I came to identify St Paul with the ferocious and highly-
lethal Saul of *Samuel* and the *Acts of the Apostles*. It
remained in my mind as the supreme historical instance of
personal metamorphosis, often serving as a comparison with
the identity changes of lesser men. The Law Reports abound
with stories of people who have carefully discarded one
identity in order to assume another; and among the various
means that they have adopted one finds instances of sudden
death, apparent suicide and unexplained disappearances on
the part of the unwanted ego.

The case of Alfred Arthur Rouse in 1931, for example,
was remarkable not only for the widespread uneasiness in
legal circles about the justness of the trial and verdict, but
also for the fact that he was said to have invested another
man, a homeless tramp, with his own identity before killing
him in circumstances that could be attributed to suicide or
accident. Rouse had the most compelling of reasons for
wanting to get rid of his familiar self and start life again
with a new one: a superfluity of mistresses, and a wife. The
anxiety of the prosecution to suggest a motive—it may
have seemed a necessity—was considered to justify the
admission, in the hearing before the magistrates, of evidence
about Rouse's women. Evidence of motive is not, however, an inescapable necessity; and it was excluded when

158

the case came before a jury. But the damage had been done: every newspaper in the country had told the story of Rouse's women, and there could have been few potential jurors who had not read it. In the result, few lawyers thought that Rouse was innocent of the murder, but fewer thought that he should have been convicted. He was hanged for killing a tramp whom he had given a lift in his car; it was said that he stunned the man, drenched the car with petrol, and burnt both car and tramp to cinders.

Rouse's case illustrates merely one of the reasons why a man sometimes identifies himself with someone else and then kills him—or seems to. But a man may sometimes think it important to merge the identities of two other persons— usually of two persons long dead. If ever it seemed important to you to prove that a pavement artist at Hyde Park Corner was really the President of the Royal Academy, it would be best to wait, if you could, until they and everyone who knew them well had died. Thereafter, you would be surprised how easy it was, unless you were too old yourself. It is a kind of exercise that has enthralled men since they first realised that you could get something extra by trickery, but it has also sustained many earnest societies concerned to prove that Peter the Painter was driving a tramcar in Melbourne, that the Crown Prince Rüpprecht of Bavaria was the rightful King of England, that 'William Shakespeare' was Christoper Marlowe, Lord Bacon, the Earl of Oxford, or Ben Jonson, that Homer was a syndicate and that Omar Khayyam never lived. Occasionally, when it has shown exceptional promise of material profit, it has sustained limited liability companies whose determination and loyalty to the cause of their promotion could be a pattern to industry.

A number of companies like this were formed in the early years of this century to prove that the first chairman of Druce's in Baker Street was really the fifth Duke of

Portland. This may seem an odd duality, but if it could be proved (and the process was bound to be expensive) there was money in it for someone; not the money of Druce and Co., Ltd., but the Portland millions, and the subsequent share-out would represent a handsome dividend on the investors' money. The proposition that 'Thomas Charles Druce' was an assumed identity of the fifth Duke of Portland, and that one of 'Mr Druce's' sons (he had two marriages and some illegitimate children) was therefore the sixth Duke of Portland, was first mooted in 1896 by his daughter-in-law, Mrs Annie Maria Druce. Even during the fifth Duke's lifetime there were rumours, fed by his eccentricity and his frequent disappearances from public life, that he was really somebody else. Once it was alleged that he had hidden a dead body on the roof of his house in Cavendish Square, and the story gained such wide credence that a sanitary inspector was sent to look for it. The story was no more true than the later one that he was T. C. Druce, but it was far more easily disproved.

Mrs Annie Druce was a widow, already in her sixties at the time this story begins, and one of the great 'litigants in person' of all time. Whether she herself ever really believed that her father-in-law was a Duke of Portland no one will ever know with complete certainty; and much of the respect that her story might otherwise have retained, despite all that happened to her and her claim, was dissipated by the fact that in 1904, after six years of bitter and determined litigation in almost every kind of court that administers law in this country, she ended in a mental home.

Mrs Annie Druce, who badly needed money to sustain her strange battle, and who had not yet thought of promoting a limited company on the strength of her expectations, sold her story to *Lloyd's Weekly News* on 13th March, 1898. By that time she had been in and out of the courts for two years, but this 1898 account is the first coherent and public report of her claim that can be found. 'The marriage which took place on 30th October, 1851, at New Windsor, Berkshire,' said Mrs Druce, 'between my late husband's father and mother, and in which their names are recorded as Thomas Charles Druce and Annie May, spinster, was in reality between the Marquis of Titchfield, afterwards fifth Duke of Portland, and the illegitimate daughter of the fifth Earl of Berkeley.'

It is the classic opening to many of the great primogeniture impostures of feudal history. This couple, said Mrs Druce, had lived together for many years before their marriage; and she suggested that the eccentric character of the fifth Duke of Portland, which became an important factor in the proof of his identity in the course of the Druce-Portland trials, was shown by the circumstances leading up to this love affair that had occupied him as Marquis of Titchfield. The girl in the case, Annie May, had also won the heart of his brother, Lord George Bentinck; and 'the climax to the quarrel,' said Mrs Druce, 'was reached on 21st September, 1848, when Lord George was found dead near Welbeck Abbey—it was stated from a spasm of the heart. Whether this was the true cause can now, of course, never be known; but it is quite certain that from that time my husband's father' (by which she meant the fifth Duke of Portland) 'suffered the keenest remorse and the most abject fear.'

Motive was thus established, Mrs Druce may have thought, for the destruction of one identity and the assumption of another. The frightened Duke, she said, chose the name of Druce and set up a furnishing 'bazaar' in Baker Street. 'Nearly always in a state of terror, he took various courses for his protection, and, adopting the name of Thomas Charles Druce, transferred *to* himself, as Druce, immense property *from* himself as the Duke of Portland.'

It had been one of the Duke of Portland's most talked-of eccentricities that the family seat at Welbeck Abbey, near Worksop, was equipped by him with an elaborate, and

F

apparently purposeless, system of underground passages, staircases, and rooms. 'He did precisely the same thing with the Baker Street Bazaar,' said Mrs Druce in her *Lloyd's Weekly News* statement; 'his desire in each case being that he might have always ready a place of refuge. But realising the risk of exposure to which he was exposing himself by his double existence, he determined to end his life as Druce; and for that purpose he caused a coffin to be buried with his supposed remains.'

She had plenty of proof, she said, that the Druce-Portland man was in fact not in that coffin. But 'even after this, the fifth Duke's fears were not quieted, and at last he determined to assume madness in order that, should he ever be accused of any crime, he might have the plea of insanity to fall back upon.' And there was no shortage of evidence upon which this notoriously eccentric nobleman, even more than most of us, could have been adjudged insane—although, in fact, he never was.

The story of the fake funeral could have been exposed as false—and with it the whole of Mrs Druce's story must have collapsed—if the coffin had been opened then and there. It had lain undisturbed for thirty-four years—from 1864 until 1898; but the probability that she herself implicitly believed in the truth of her story, and therefore in the validity of her son's claim to the Portland millions, is suggested by the dogged determination with which she set about the legal Odyssey of getting the grave opened.

She was opposed at every step of the way by the Druce family; and, as you may imagine, she was not encouraged by the Duke of Portland's family. In 1896 she applied to the Home Secretary for an exhumation order, authorising the opening of a coffin in one of the vaults of Highgate Cemetery, which purported to be that of Thomas Charles Druce. In her petition she set out that she was the widow of Walter Thomas Druce (T. C. Druce's son), that T.C. had not died in 1864, when the 'mock' funeral took place, and that the coffin did not contain his body. The Home Secretary was asked to believe that the reason for this desecration of Highgate Cemetery was that 'T. C. Druce' was merely the adopted name of the fifth Duke of Portland, William John Cavendish Bentinck-Scott, and that when the Duke had got tired of his assumed identity as a Baker Street shopkeeper he had got rid of it by way of a mock funeral and burial.

The Home Office is a sceptical Department of State. It told Mrs Druce that she must take the matter before the courts and allow the normal processes of evidence to show whether Home Office intervention was warranted.

She tried the Highgate Cemetery authorities. Ask the Home Office, they said. She went to the House of Lords, which coldly sent her away to get her case properly prepared and presented by counsel. She asked the Bow Street Magistrate, who had no jurisdiction in the matter. But it must, Mrs Druce decided, be within someone's jurisdiction: surely you could break into this circle somewhere? The Bishop of London—a false burial—desecration of consecrated ground—that made it a matter for the ecclesiastical courts? The Bishop was more helpful. The Chancellor of the Diocese was the man, he said, who dealt with that kind of thing.

The Chancellor of the Diocese of London was Dr T. H. Tristram, Q.C. Declining to deal with Mrs Druce's application 'in chambers,' he directed that the case should be heard in full Consistory Court. On 9th March, 1898, that court assembled in St Paul's Cathedral, and for the first time this virtually penniless woman (borrowing £20 from the *Daily Mail* for her expenses) was able to state her case before a tribunal which admitted competency to do something about it. She wanted a faculty, she said, for an examination of 'T. C. Druce's' open coffin. The vault in which it had lain since 1864 had been opened in 1880, when her own husband, Walter Thomas Druce, was buried, his coffin being placed on top of his father's. It was opened again in 1893, to bury

T.C. Druce's widow; and it was then found that Walter Thomas Druce's coffin had dropped in the vault 'to such an extent as to show that the coffin below it, his father's, was empty.'

She told them the story of the mock funeral. The coffin had been filled with 200 lb. of lead, to simulate the weight of a human body. There was a funeral procession of fifty carriages, filled with assistants from Druce's shop, which wound its way round the streets of North London (said Mrs Druce) and finished up nowhere—certainly not at a cemetery or a funeral service. There is no record of the shop assistants' feelings, or of how they were kept quiet about this funeral that never was. But to set the seal of verisimilitude upon her story, let me quote the judgment delivered in due course by the Chancellor of the Diocese of London:

'This is an application of an unusual nature,' said Dr Tristram, 'but one not without precedent. It is for a faculty authorising the opening of a family vault or brick grave in the consecrated portion of Highgate Cemetery, and for the temporary removal from out of the vault of the two uppermost coffins, for the purpose of ascertaining whether the third and lowest coffin, which had been placed there in December, 1864, purporting by the death and burial certificates to contain the body of Thomas Charles Druce, really contained any body at all. The suggestion made by the petitioner, who is his daughter-in-law, is that the burial was a fictitious one; that the person who is represented in the death and burial registers to have been buried in December, 1864, was seen alive some years afterwards; and that the fictitious burial was planned in order to palm off his feigned death and burial on his only legitimate son—then of the age of twelve years—so as to enable the will of the living man to be proved or his property to fall under control of persons to the son's detriment.

'The court has jurisdiction,' Dr Tristram went on, 'to grant the application, and it is its duty to do so, provided it is satisfied that the applicants have or may have an interest in the estate of Thomas Charles Druce, that they are desirous of taking action in the civil courts to protect their interests in his estate, and that the information they may obtain by the granting of the faculty may be of service to them in such action. The petitioner has satisfied the court that she has an interest in the estate of her father-in-law, because she is a representative of the son; the son certainly had an interest in the estate under the will; and she, as his representative, may have a further interest in ascertaining whether the property has been properly and legitimately administered. She has satisfied me on that important point.

'It certainly is a very curious case; but what strikes the court is that the certificate of death does not contain the name of the medical gentleman who purported to certify the cause of death. That is a very serious omission.' (It was also one of the least emphasised and yet most important details in the whole case that T. C. Druce's 1864 'burial' was a fake.) 'He was buried only three days after his death, and his son, who was then twelve, was not present at the funeral but heard of it.

'In these circumstances,' the Chancellor concluded, 'the court is prepared to decree a faculty to issue, authorising this lady, who has an interest in the matter, and who is anxious to take proceedings in the civil courts for the protection of her own interests and her son's interests in the property of Thomas Charles Druce, to have the vault opened, the two coffins temporarily removed, and an investigation made as to whether the lowest coffin, which purports to contain the body of Thomas Charles Druce, contains any body at all.'

That could have been the end of the affair. But the Chancellor added to his judgment an injunction that 'persons who have an adverse interest must be given notice of this, and be allowed to attend. The vault will be opened, and some

officials of the cemetery will attend. There should be some
independent persons present to give evidence.' Among the
persons with an 'adverse interest' to Mrs Druce's was her
brother-in-law, Herbert Druce. She had married a Druce
who was born in wedlock, but Herbert Druce, the eldest
son of T. C., was born before his father married. Herbert
accordingly had a strong interest in the safeguarding of T.
C's existing will, since it treated all the brothers and sisters as
legitimate. Any possibility that the Highgate tomb did not
contain the body of T. C. Druce (and who could say what
chicanery had been going on, in view of the fantastic stories
now being told?) might lead to the invalidation of his will
and to an intestacy that would have left Herbert Druce out
in the cold.

Herbert therefore opposed the opening of the grave with
rather more than the natural repugnance anyone would
display in a similar situation. He joined forces with T. C.
Druce's executors and with other members of the family
to obtain leave from the Chancellor of the London Diocese
to intervene in the suit, and to postpone the opening of the
grave pending a fuller enquiry. This enquiry took the form
of a High Court application for a writ of prohibition, pre-
venting the opening of the grave; and although it failed,
someone discovered in the course of the hearing that there
would have to be a licence from the Home Secretary before
the grave could be opened at all.

Up to now Mrs Annie Druce was slightly over on the
winning side. But it was rather half-heartedly that she went
back to the Chancellor of the Diocese to get her grave-
opening faculty renewed, for she had had nearly enough of
the ecclesiastics; and this time she joined with her name that
of her son, Sidney George Druce, to show that her own
interest was not without altruistic qualities. She was now
setting greater store by an action that came on in the Probate
Division of the High Court on 8th August, 1898 (five months
after the Consistory Court in St Paul's) to do just what

Herbert Druce dreaded most—revoke the will of T. C. Druce and leave the illegitimate Herbert disinherited. This was tried by Sir Francis Jeune, President of the Probate Division, and it had already been arranged during the second hearing before the Chancellor of the Diocese of London that the ecclesiastical issue should be settled once for all by merging, for this occasion, the two jurisdictions. Mr Justice Jeune thought the grave ought to be opened, because that would settle the matter of the will. He made an order accordingly, but confounded everyone present by inviting any aggrieved party to appeal against it, and declaring that no more was to be done in the matter pending any such appeal. Off went Herbert and his supporters to the Court of Appeal only to find that it declined jurisdiction in the matter. Mr Justice Jeune's decision was not an order for exhumation, said the Court of Appeal: it was an opinion that the Consistory Court ought really to hear Mrs Druce's application—and grant it. You couldn't appeal in the Court of Appeal against that. Costs against Herbert Druce and T. C's executors.

Back went Mrs Druce to the Chancellor of the Diocese of London, obtaining a fresh faculty to open the grave. The other side at once gave notice of appeal; but in the meantime the Home Office had been talking to the Law Officers of the Crown, and they suddenly told the cemetery company (probably because the cemetery company asked them) that no grave could be opened without a licence from the Home Secretary. When the cemetery company passed on this information to Mrs Druce, she went back to the Consistory Court and asked the Chancellor to summon the cemetery company before him, requiring an explanation of their defiance. He arranged a special sitting for 21st December, 1898, at which the company would have to explain how a Home Office letter could take precedence over a joint order of the Probate Division and a Consistory Court. But on the day before the hearing the cemetery authority persuaded a Queen's Bench Court to stay all further proceedings.

That is a part skeleton of the kind of litigation that had now lasted for two and a half years and was to go on for another two. In 1900 Mrs Druce's activities were still filling the newspapers—an action against the London Cemetery Company claiming the monetary value of the Druce family grave, because they were refusing her access to it and it was really her son's property; then another application to Mr Justice Jeune, who had once come down on her side, for an order that the grave should be opened. For one technical reason or another, she always failed; and although it is a matter of record that she always seemed to enlist the sympathy of the Judges, it seems highly probable that she would never, in fact, have got Home Office permission to open the grave.

'Why not open it?' everyone was asking, for the story had been public property now for years, 'featured' and grotesquely headlined in newspapers all over the world. *Lloyd's Weekly News* had followed up Mrs Druce's long and factual statement of her case (see page 160) with a leading article on 27th March, 1898, that said:

> The growing opinion is that nothing but exhumation can afford a solution of this strange case. The remark heard on every hand is: 'If Mrs Druce be a deluded lady, why not have this straightaway proved by opening the grave and the coffin therein? The spade would speedily settle the vexed question.' But it is not the intention of the solicitors of the trustees of the will to have that tomb disturbed. Indeed the eagerness of Mrs Druce in the direction of exhumation is only equalled by their eagerness to prevent her. An impartial public naturally infers that Mrs Druce's contention gives her opponents an uneasy feeling of uncertainty as to the contents of that coffin, lowered into the vault thirty-four years ago, and purporting to hold the remains of the late Thomas Charles Druce, her husband's father.

And on 17th August, 1898, the *Daily Mail* joined in:

> Surely if the vault is taking all these months to open, the lawyers can spend another year or two on the new crop of arguments which the opening of the vault will suggest before the contents of the coffin are revealed. After the coffin is opened—but that brings us, apparently, to the twentieth century, and further speculation would seem a trifle premature. Mrs Druce's prediction that her son will be 'Duke of Portland by Christmas' stands little chance of verification, even if the lady meant Christmas, 2000.

It was for the *Weekly Dispatch*, however, to outdo the Press of the world with a report on 26th February, 1899, that eliminated the valiant figure of Mrs Druce and brought others on to the stage in her place. T. C. Druce, it declared, had been married before, in 1816. He had a son by this earlier marriage, of whom there was a living descendant in the person of George Hollamby Druce, who throughout these years of litigation had been mining in Australia—in apparent oblivion as to the story that had been entertaining the rest of the world. If, therefore, T. C. Druce's will could be revoked, George Hollamby Druce of Australia (and not Mrs Annie Druce and her son) would have first claim upon his estate, whether that estate was the Baker Street shop or the Portland millions. He came on the scene with an application, through counsel in the High Court, to get Mrs Druce's litigious activities stalled for six months; but as things turned out, the collapse and disappearance of poor Mrs Druce, made inevitable by the advent of this new claimant (whom she denounced in vain as an impostor), was followed by about six years of almost complete silence, and the Druce-Portland case began to fade from the public mind.

Then, in 1905, the limited companies began to blossom. First G. H. Druce, Ltd., share capital £11,000, made up of ten thousand one pound shares and twenty thousand at a shilling, all held by G. H. Druce—but half of them sold in the course of the next two years. Then in 1907, the Druce-Portland Company, Ltd., and the New Druce-Portland Company, Ltd. All these promotions were concerned with the profits to be shared when the Portland millions were safely in the bag, and George Hollamby Druce was the subscribers' fancy. 'If George Hollamby Druce should prove successful in his claims,' said one of the prospectuses, addressing a British public that had come to accept the Druce-Portland saga as a later generation was to accept flying saucers and interplanetary flight debentures, 'this company would be entitled to a sum equal to ten per cent of the whole, or £1,600,000. In other words, each 5s. share of this company would receive £16, or sixty-four times the amount subscribed.' It was the heyday of the limited liability company: people put their resources into any scheme that promised a good return, and the great fortunes of the aristocratic houses were still available for redistribution among people who knew what wealth was for. The money poured in. George Hollamby Druce was not likely to be defeated, as Mrs Annie Druce was, by lack of funds. Not merely was he in possession of something like £100,000 of publicly-subscribed money: he was not going to embark on any stand-up fight in the High Court with the great Portland family, which could brush off £100,000 as if it were a fly. (The Portland family were said to have offered £50,000 even to Mrs Druce, years before, to drop the case—not because her claim had the slightest foundation, but because Danegeld sometimes leaves you with a lot more of your money than justice does.) On the contrary: G. H. Druce was going to thrash it all out in the criminal courts, by the simple expedient of prosecuting the unfortunate Herbert Druce, who had steadily and wearily told the truth throughout these years of infuriating litigation, for perjury.

If Mrs Annie Druce (now safely off the scene) had been

right in her claim that T. C. Druce was never buried in that coffin, then Herbert Druce was a liar; he had sworn on oath, repeatedly, that he actually saw his father's body in it. For the new claimant, this was an attractive gambit: a perjury prosecution could entail two full hearings, one before a magistrate and another before a jury, and then perhaps an appeal. All the whole story could be dragged out over and over again, through and through the courts and the newspapers; and all the cost of the prosecution would be borne by the Crown. It is a well-proved method of getting dormant issues retried, and the cheapest by far.

The perjury prosecution began and ended in Marylebone Magistrates' Court, lasting fourteen days, which were spread over the ten weeks from 25th October, 1907, to 6th January, 1908. The evidence disclosed a huge and involved conspiracy, inculpating more and more people; building up a mighty edifice of lies and fantasies; bringing witnesses from America, Australia, India, Ireland; introducing the names of famous and blameless people who would have detested the whole affair—Charles Dickens and Sir Morell Mackenzie among them; until at last, on 16th December, 1907, the magistrate, Mr Chichele Plowden, hinted very strongly that although no one could compel Mr Herbert Druce, the prisoner, to allow the opening of the grave, 'it would be a very desirable step to take in the interests of justice.' Herbert·Druce may well have thought, by now, that further refusal to open the grave might indeed land him in prison for a perjury he had never committed.

After these ten years of stubborn refusal, therefore, he gave way to the overwhelming opinion against him and agreed to the opening of the grave. Accordingly, during the actual currency of the perjury trial, yet another Consistory Court assembled in St Paul's Cathedral. The Home Secretary had already granted an exhumation licence at Herbert Druce's instance, and the Consistory Court formally granted yet

another faculty for the opening of the grave. *The Times* of
31st December, 1907, described the scene that so many
readers had been waiting for:

> Before dawn yesterday morning a small group of men
> had taken possession of seats opposite to the main gates
> of Highgate Cemetery. The biting wind which swept the
> northern heights, carrying before it now rain, now cutting
> particles of sleet, did not deter the curious among the
> public, and by daylight the attendance had appreciably
> grown. As early as five o'clock the main gates were
> opened to let in the electricians who were responsible
> for the completion of the special electric lighting arrange-
> ments. Two hours later a covered van drove up in charge
> of men who were bringing the necessary tools for opening
> the coffin. Three other vehicles arrived later, conveying
> several of the official personages authorised by Dr
> Tristram . . .

Dr Tristram, it will be rememberd, was the Chancellor
of the Diocese. There is in this spacious contemporary
report, starting in the small hours and in the dark, a skilful
crescendo in which Dr Tristram's personages mark the onset
of real excitement. But there was then a long wait,
until . . .

> At 10.20 Dr Pepper, the representative of the Home
> Office, Sir Thomas Stevenson, and a surveyor representing
> Mr Herbert Druce put in an appearance. Other arrivals
> were Chief Inspector Dew* and Sir Melville Macnaghten,
> Assistant Commissioner of Police.

Shortly after this Mr George Hollamby Druce turned up,
was refused admission to the enclosure, protested, and went
away. He had already rather lost status, and his sands were
running out fast. But there are people still living who profess

---

* Who remembers him now as the man who arrested Dr. Crippen on his
way to New York?

to believe that his own faith in his claim was genuine, even if it was the product of gullibility, cupidity, and mistrust.

The *Times* reporter goes next into a detailed account of the digging, the removing of the 'great flagstone' from the tomb with crowbars and rollers, and the raising of the coffin. He continues:

> The name-plate having been washed, the inscription became plainly visible:
>
> Thomas Charles Druce
> Esqre
> Died 28th Decr
> 1864
> In his 71st year.
>
> Above and below the inscription was a brass cross. A photograph was taken . . . the lid was removed, bringing away with it the top of the innermost wooden shell which was attached to it. Then there was displayed a shrouded human figure which proved to be that of an aged, bearded man.

At the next (and last) hearing in the Magistrates' Court, Mr Pepper—the Bernard Spilsbury of his day—gave evidence of the exhumation and said that the body in the coffin bore a 'striking resemblance' to the photograph of T. C. Druce. One of T. C. Druce's partners in the Baker Street business said that he, too, saw the body, and recognised it 'beyond a shadow of doubt—there is no doubt whatever about it.'

The prosecution, in the person of Mr Atherley-Jones, K.C., M.P., dropped the case. 'I would like to say that why I have come to this conclusion, not further to proceed in this case,' said Mr Atherley Jones, 'is that the theory of the prosecution undoubtedly was, not only that Mr Thomas Charles Druce and the Duke of Portland were one and the same person, but that this funeral was a sham funeral, not on the theory of any suppositious body, but that they put some material in the coffin, and it was conveyed away from the bazaar under pretence of a death having occurred, apparently to Highgate Cemetery. It is impossible for me to proceed with the prosecution when there has been demonstrated in the clearest and most complete manner that the death *did* take place at Hendon, that the body *was* interred at Highgate Cemetery, and that the body which has been now exhumed is the same body as that which was then interred—and when undoubtedly very strong identification of that body as that of the late Thomas Charles Druce has been given. And I should be acting entirely contrary to the best traditions of my profession if I were to proceed in the face of that evidence.'

The remarks then made by the magistrate, Mr Chichele Plowden, have some claim to immortality:

No one can now doubt that Thomas Charles Druce existed in fact; that he died in his own home in the midst of his family; and that he was buried in due course in the family vault in the cemetery at Highgate. His existence stands out as clear, as distinct, and as undeniable as that of any human being that ever lived. How the myth ever arose that confused him and the fifth Duke of Portland as the same personality it would be idle to speculate. Sufficient to say that this case is an illustration of that love of the marvellous which is so deeply ingrained in legal annals as affording one more striking proof of the unfathomable depths of human credulity.

Mr Plowden then turned to Mr Atherley-Jones, who had conducted the prosecution throughout with skill and acerbity in almost equal proportions, calling a series of witnesses who, to his obvious distress but in no way to his personal discredit, now stood exposed as perjurers in their turn:

The summons is dismissed (said the magistrate), if that

is the right form to take. It amounts to the same thing whether you withdraw your summons or I dismiss it. I have only one final word to say. Mr Herbert Druce leaves this court with his character for truthfulness absolutely and conclusively vindicated. I think that he also deserves the acknowledgment of the court for having consented to take a course which, though it may have materially served his defence, was nevertheless in the highest degree distasteful—and I think rightly and naturally so—to his feelings as a son and as a Christian gentleman.

The reverberations went on for a long time. There were the limited companies to wind up, the shareholders, cheated of their claim on the Portland millions, to be paid out. They got a very small return for their money, though they may well have accepted this with the fortitude that sustains football pool promoters today. The leading liar in the case was an elderly Irish-born American quack doctor named Robert Caldwell, who said that he was introduced to the Duke of Portland in 1864 by Sir Morell Mackenzie at Welbeck Abbey, the seat of the Portland family. The Duke suffered from a skin disease that gave him a bulbous nose, and Caldwell, who claimed to have cured himself of a similar affliction some years before, relieved the Duke of some thousands of pounds in fees for curing him similarly. It was he who 'saw' the mock funeral later that same year, 'saw' the lead put into the empty coffin, and actually helped to put the lid on and screw it down. The whole of his evidence was amazingly circumstantial. He stood up to days of examination and cross-examination until Mr Horace Avory, for the defence, began to involve him in the inevitable web of sub-lies and rationalisations that can usually be spun for the perjurer; and then, in one of the intervals between the magisterial hearings, he suddenly ran away to America and was never heard of again.

Another of the witnesses was less fortunate. This was

Miss Mary Robinson, an American lady who had come to this country to avoid the rigours of the Civil War, and who met T. C. Druce socially from time to time, then became his amanuensis, and soon became aware (she asserted) that he was really the Duke of Portland. After the collapse of the Herbert Druce perjury case, she herself was, fairly enough, indicted for perjury; and at the Old Bailey on 10th April, 1908, Mr Justice Walton sentenced her to four years' penal servitude. In Holloway Prison, on remand, she had written a full confession describing a world-wide conspiracy to milk the Portland family by diligently fostering the whole fantastic story of personation and transferred identity.

What the Marylebone Magistrate had called 'that love of the marvellous which is so deeply ingrained in human nature' can, in short, always be called into action by any plausible appeal to the mystery of human identity. In cases like the Druce-Portland story it can inflict untold and lasting injury on its victims—in this case two whole families with nothing in common save inheritable property and one member each with a reputation for eccentricity. And what the magistrate called 'the unfathomable depths of human credulity' are specially susceptible to the crystallising processes of the law. Once the statement of a belief, or the deliberately false assertion of a profitable untruth, is enshrined in an affidavit, a statement of claim, or a deposition, scepticism is in full retreat. The law itself must take its share of the blame for this: 'it is impossible to hold that there are no such things as witches,' said Lord Chief Justice Hale, 'since there are laws against witches, and it is not conceivable that laws should be made against that which does not exist.' It was a dictum which, in an age of dawning reason and humanity, probably sent a few hundred more helpless old women to their deaths. The law had spoken, its stamp of truth was upon what many people might otherwise have begun to doubt. The writs in the Druce-Portland case have a powerful air of verisimilitude, and Mrs Druce's unshakable persistence, so far as popular opinion was concerned, did nearly all that was necessary to win genuine support. What little more was needed was supplied by the Druce family's refusal to open their private grave to satisfy cranks, impostors, scribblers and the mob. Why should they open it? Personal identity is a precious thing. This was a case in which it was considered to be worth hundreds of thousands of pounds.

XI

ROGER TICHBORNE

Nᴏᴛ all the famous cases of disputed identity have involved fraud, and in some of them the dispute is likely to remain for ever unresolved. Sometimes there has been no question of *lucri causa,* the motive varying from delusions of grandeur, as in the case of 'Henriette de Bourbon," to a concern for the gaiety of nations, as in the case of the immortal Horace Cole.

The former was a dignified young seventeenth century Frenchwoman who, taking advantage of the absence in England of Queen Henrietta Maria (the sister of Louis XIII and the bride of Charles I of England) assumed that lady's identity with unexpected and inexplicable success in the Limoges district of France in the early years of the seventeenth century. The real Henrietta Maria was living in London as Charles I's consort. The impostor carried off the impersonation with such grace and *hauteur* that for some time everyone accepted her as a royal personage. She had in fact a royal time, and one can only hope that it compensated her for the whipping and imprisonment that followed her exposure by a commission of enquiry sent down at last from Paris.

Horace Cole was inspired by the brilliant success of the 'Captain of Koepernick.' This was, as it happens, an impersonation that did involve a fraud, but the manner and nature of it belong to a past that it is impossible not to envy. In 1896 an ex-convict named William Voigt acquired, somehow or other, the uniform of a captain in the First Prussian Guards, collected a party of a dozen duped but genuine

Guardsmen, strutted into the Town Hall of Koepernick (a suburb of Berlin), confiscated the funds of the municipal treasury, arrested the burgomaster and the treasurer, and sent them under military escort to Berlin. Not even his consequent four years' imprisonment has ever dimmed his lustre. Many years later Mr Adrian Stephen, the brother of Virginia Woolf, was planning a similar exploit. 'Of all the institutions in the world,' he wrote,* 'that offered a leg for everyone's pulling, the most obvious was the German Army':

My suggestion was simply that Cole and I should acquire the uniforms of German officers and take them with us to some town near the Franco-German frontier in Alsace-Lorraine. We were to choose a suitable neighbourhood for the purpose and then, putting on our uniforms, to take command of a detachment of troops and march with them across the frontier into France. Once we got across, what happened would naturally have depended on circumstances. I had no doubt, of course, that the French would stop us before we had gone a kilometre. We should have surrendered immediately, and perhaps been interned; there would, I hoped, have been what is called an 'international incident,' the Kaiser would have made gestures and sent telegrams, and other people might have been amused . . . I do not know that if everyone shared my feelings towards the great armed forces of the world, the world would not be a happier place to live in.'

But Horace Cole preferred to impersonate the Sultan of Zanzibar and pay a State visit to Cambridge.

The Druce-Portland story (page 158) is evidence enough of the romantic excitement that you can exploit in the public mind by laying claim to a title, but the feudal history of England abounds in such stories. Consider the cases of Richard Cook, the bogus Lord Stafford, of 1824, and

* *The Dreadnought Hoax*, Hogarth Press, 1936.

Thomas Purvis, who sought the baronetcy of Sir Hugh Smyth in 1852. Cook was one of the last offenders to commit the crime called 'forcible entry and detainer': he collected a band of followers, forcibly claimed the Stafford barony, stormed the castle, and collected the estate rents. He hired a four-horsed carriage bearing the Stafford arms, made a triumphal and gracious entry into the town of Stafford, and enjoyed a crowded hour, the end of which he must have had clearly in mind throughout the escapade. Purvis, on the other hand, went about his claim to the baronetcy and estates of Ashton Hall, in Gloucestershire, by the more peaceful but equally hazardous method of carefully hatched perjury. When his action against Sir Hugh Smyth came on in 1853, it broke down at the point (he must surely have foreseen it?) where an interview he was describing as having taken place between himself and Lady Bath was shown to coincide with a time when he was in prison for stealing a horse. He got twenty-one years.

Such cases may be cited from among a host of others to set the stage for the greatest identity puzzle that has ever come before the English Courts: the Tichborne Claimant.

Roger Charles Tichborne was born in Paris on 5th January, 1829. He was the eldest son of James Francis Doughty-Tichborne, the tenth baronet, and Henriette, the illegitimate daughter of Henry Seymour of Knoyle, in Wiltshire. He lived in France, learning no English, until he was sixteen, and then came to England, to 'finish' at Stonyhurst College. Then for three and a half years he was an officer in the Sixth Dragoon Guards. When he was twenty-four years old he became secretly engaged to his cousin; and then, either because this failed to meet with her father's approval, or because he was unhappy at home anyway (the accounts of this vary), he took the unusual course of getting on to a ship, sailing for Valparaiso, and crossing the Andes to Rio de Janeiro. His fiancée's father died while he was there, and, possibly with

the intention of returning home, he sailed from Rio for
Australia on 20th April, 1854, in a vessel called the *Bella*
which was wrecked and sunk with all hands a few days later.
His will was proved, legal proof was given of his death, and
the insurances on his life were paid out.

His mother, Lady Tichborne, like so many tragic mothers
before and since, absolutely refused to accept the notion of
his death. She began a systematic campaign of advertising,
seeking information about Roger Tichborne throughout the
world. Year after year she thus persisted, despite the general
assumption, inside and outside the Tichborne family, that
Roger was dead. This advertisement, which appeared in
The Times of 14th May, 1863, in English, French, and
Spanish, was typical of them all:

> If anybody can give any clue of
> ROGER CHARLES TICHBORNE, and
> if there are any survivors of *La
> Bella,* they are requested to let
> L. T. know of them, at 1,
> Nottingham Place, Regent's
> Park. A handsome REWARD is
> promised for any well-authen-
> ticated particulars.

It is, of course, an open invitation to the crook. There are
people who study the newspapers for precisely such opportunities: the personal identity game plus the long-lost heir
plus a mother's grief make up a combination that few crooks
can resist. It is a risk that the advertiser takes, for a response
might possibly come from an honest person. You are indeed
quite likely to find someone who thinks, or can soon be
persuaded by others to think, that he is the person you seek.
And you might even find the real man. For many years,
every hard-up merchant seaman found a welcome at 1
Nottingham Place or at Tichborne Park. And then one of
the advertisements, thirteen years after the loss of *La Bella,*

came to the notice of a Mr William Gibbes, a solicitor at Wagga-Wagga, in New South Wales, who seems to have believed that Roger Tichborne was living there and working as a butcher, in the name of Castro. He wrote to Lady Tichborne and said so. Funds were at once provided, and 'Castro' sailed for England.

When Lady Tichborne saw him, she knew and welcomed him at once. She later swore an affidavit that in him she recognised her long-lost son; and she allowed him £1,000 a year to sustain him until his identity, which the rest of the Tichborne family angrily disputed, could be established in a court of law.

Meanwhile the Tichborne family got busy. They obtained evidence that 'Castro' was identical with Arthur Orton, the son of an East London butcher, who had deserted a sailing ship at Valparaiso in 1850 and had been hospitably looked after for some weeks by a family named Castro at the town of Melipilla, in Chile. Orton, for reasons which no one seems to have discovered, adopted the name of Castro when he later lived in New South Wales. Here then were the foundations of a three-cornered identity wrangle that cost something like a quarter of a million pounds in legal expenses, lasted for many years, divided the people of England into excited and avidly-interested factions, and chased the Franco-Prussian War from the front pages of the newspapers.

The trials began in May, 1871, with an ejectment suit by Castro-Orton-Tichborne, whom I am henceforth going to call 'the Claimant,' against a Colonel Lushington, who was then the tenant of Tichborne Park. The real defendants of course were the Tichborne family, personified for the moment in the infant Henry Tichborne, possessor of the estates. When the case moved into the Court of Common Pleas, the special jury caused quite a lot of preliminary trouble. They had an idea—as almost everyone had—that

this trial was likely to last many months. A lot of jurors
summoned therefore failed to turn up, preferring to pay
a fine for non-attendance; and those who did turn up wanted
handsome payment for their services. As it was, the case
was tried by a jury of eleven, at a rate of pay, agreed on by
both sides, that put all previous and all subsequent juries in
the shade.

As the case went on, numerous side-issues emerged to
make it the most complicated, as well as by far the longest,
trial in legal history. It is significant that both Serjeant
Ballantine, who represented the Claimant in the civil actions,
and Dr Edward Kenealy, Q.C., who defended him on the
subsequent perjury charges, believed from first to last that
he was the rightful heir to the Tichborne estates. It is
probable that millions of people were brought to the same
belief by the end of the trials. But the Claimant failed in
the civil courts, after a trial lasting one hundred and three
days; and he was then indicted and convicted of perjury—
firstly in swearing that he was Roger Tichborne and secondly
in denying on oath that he was Arthur Orton—and was
sentenced to fourteen years' penal servitude.

I am not concerned here with the conduct of the two
trials, which seems to have come fairly near to the lowest
level of disorder and injustice in English legal history. (Dr
Kenealy himself was subsequently disbarred for saying so.)
Nor could the true merits of the Tichborne case be
adequately presented in anything smaller than an encylo-
pedia. This is a book about the perils and benefits of
personal identity, and the ways in which they can respectively
be avoided and enjoyed; and for that reason I quote here,
first, an extract from Serjeant Ballantine's book *Some
Experiences of a Barrister's Life.*

    I propose to show what weapons the representatives
of Sir Roger Tichborne's family possessed to counter the
attack. In the first place they were entitled to, and did as

a matter of fact, file affidavits; and in them might have given—and ought, in my opinion, to have done—any information they possessed bearing upon the facts. Some five or six years afterwards *they alleged for the first time that the real Sir Roger had indelible tattoo marks upon one of his arms, of which they were aware when he first made his claim, but nothing was then said in the affidavits on this subject.*

Now the Claimant was not tattooed at all; so that his imposture could have been exposed in a moment by asking him to show his tattoo marks. The failure of the Tichborne family to require this simple test is accepted by most students of the case as proof, not necessarily that the Claimant was right, but that the family and their legal advisers were resorting to any conceivable trick, fair or foul, perjury or truth, to prove him wrong. Three witnesses for the prosecution in the perjury trial showed the Court what the tattoo marks were like: first, Lord Bellew, who actually did the tattooing (said he) at Stoneyhurst College, when he and Roger Tichborne were boys; secondly, Lady Doughty, who was the boy's aunt; and thirdly, M. Adrian Chatillon, who was his French tutor. Except that their drawings each contained a cross, a heart, and an anchor (which most tattoo designs do, and which the witnesses could well have agreed upon) they were remarkably dissimilar and unconvincing.

The only reason (Serjeant Ballantine goes on) that I have been given for this mode of conducting the case was that the Claimant might have created the marks if he had been informed of their existence. This is nonsense: such an attempt must have been discovered and would have wrecked the case. If he had been asked the question, and attempted to shuffle, he would have been simply told to hold out his arm, and the non-existence of any such marks would have been destructive to his claim.

Assuming that this fact was really known, and that it had been proved, I have no hesitation in expressing my belief that neither the solicitor nor counsel concerned for the Claimant would have consented to go on with the case. I am confident that it would have more than shaken the belief of his warmest supporters, and, unlike those discrepancies which were abundantly proved at the trial, there would have been something palpable for common minds to grasp. And I believe this monster trial, with its gigantic bill of costs, would have perished at its birth in the Court of Chancery.

It was the 'tattoo evidence' that brought the civil proceedings to a close. The jury, which seems to have been a very talkative jury, made this fact generally known in and around the court. On the hundred-and-third day of the trial the foreman suddenly got up and said the jury had heard enough. The Attorney-General then announced that he still had two hundred and sixty witnesses to call for the Tichborne family: he had so far called only seventeen. But the jury had heard eighty-five witnesses swear that the Claimant was truthfully Sir Roger Tichborne—Lady Tichborne (his mother), the family solicitor, the family doctor, his cousin, six magistrates, one general, three colonels, one major, two captains, thirty-six N.C.O.s, four clergymen, seven tenants on the Tichborne Estate, sixteen servants of the family, and about a dozen miscellaneous witnesses. And the jury decided, in effect, that these were all perjurers. The Claimant was committed for trial as their ringleader, on an indictment for perjury.

Whereas the Claimant had attempted, in the Court of Common Pleas, to establish that he was Roger Tichborne, he was now faced with a charge not only of not being Roger Tichborne, but of being Arthur Orton.

The idea that he was Arthur Orton seems, on an examination of the evidence, sufficiently absurd to provide the plot for a comic opera; but several contemporary accounts of the trial suggest that the comic opera spirit had indeed taken hold of everyone but the prisoner and those defending him. Arthur Orton was the youngest of the twelve children of George Orton, butcher, of 69 High Street, Wapping. He suffered from St Vitus' Dance, and was a delicate boy constantly worried over by his parents. A sea trip was arranged for him in a sailing ship whose master was a friend of Mr Orton's, and his health seemed so improved that he was apprenticed, as soon as he was fourteen, to a merchant navy captain bound for Valparaiso. There he quarrelled with the captain, deserted the ship, and wandered into the interior of Chile. It was maintained by some witnesses at the trials that he was then given lodging and friendship by a Chilean cattle and provision dealer named Don Tomas Castro, in the village of Melipilla. Now the Claimant certainly said in his first two affidavits that he, the Claimant, had stayed with the Castros at Melipilla; but it was believed by the Claimant's supporters that the Tichborne family's ingenuity alone was responsible for the story that Orton had stayed there too.

At all events, after twenty months in Chile, Orton came back to England and lived in Wapping with his father until a family quarrel drove him abroad again. He went this time to Hobart Town, Tasmania, and it was from there that he was said to have written numerous letters to a girl in Wapping named Mary Ann Loder. All these letters, signed Arthur Orton, and painstakingly illiterate, were produced by the prosecution at the Claimant's perjury trial as proof of Arthur Orton's intimate acquaintance with Miss Loder; and Miss Loder was produced as a witness to the fact that Arthur Orton was in fact the Claimant. It was all very carefully, if obviously, worked out; but there seems to have arisen very soon a general belief that these letters were all forgeries, and it must be admitted that a close study of them shows them to be the kind of letters that most educated persons imagine an illiterate person would write. They are in this respect about as convincing as the phoneticised 'Cockney' speeches in Shaw's *Pygmalion*.

But physical appearances must always be paramount in questions of disputed identity. In those days, although the science of finger prints was just knocking at the door, there was no accepted method of establishing absolute uniqueness. Accordingly, the following detailed comparisons might have been thought of the utmost importance, though there is little evidence in the various accounts of the trials that they were ever properly considered. In a criminal trial that lasted for ten months (with a Long Vacation intervening) this would not be due to any lack of time:

The Tichborne Claimant	Arthur Orton
Height 5ft. 9in.	Height 5ft. 9½in.
Hair dark brown, almost black	Hair red
Eyes dark blue	Eyes light blue
Clear complexion (had not had small pox).	Heavily pockmarked
'K-legged'	Straight legs
Genitalia grotesquely malformed	Normal
Brown birthmark on left side	No birthmarks
Left thumb malformed	Normal
Never wore earrings	Ears pierced for earrings
Left eyelid punctured by fish-hook.	Normal
Wound over right eyebrow	None
No facial scars	Scar on left cheek
No tattoo mark ever mentioned until the trials.	Tattooed on both arms
Surgical blood-letting punctures on both ankles	None

The Claimant was proved by Dr David Wilson, on the 123rd day of the trial in the Court of Common Pleas, to have an 'extraordinary malformation' of the genitalia, 'such as probably would not be found in a million men.' Numerous members of the Orton family proved that Arthur Orton had no such defect; and the completeness of this dissociation in the two identities was therefore similarly, and as incontrovertibly, established as in the case of Adolf Beck (see page 76).

It was the more astonishing that precisely the same malformation of the genitalia was known to have existed in the case of Roger Tichborne, and to have caused him the utmost misery and embarrassment as a boy and as a subaltern in the Dragoon Guards. Lady Tichborne was a Frenchwoman, whose desire that her son should be brought up as a Frenchman had always come between her and the Tichbornes; and when she identified the Claimant as her son in 1867, she was subjected to prolonged and indignant pressure from the Tichborne family to retract her statement and admit that she must be mistaken. Instead she induced the Claimant to submit to a medical inspection, which afforded 'positive and conclusive evidence,' banishing from her mind all possible doubt that he was her son. This was her affidavit, sworn on 27 June, 1867:

> I am as certain as I am of my own existence, and do distinctly and positively swear, that the plaintiff (the Claimant) is my first-born son, the issue of my marriage with Sir James Francis Doughty Tichborne (deceased). His features, disposition, and voice are unmistakable, and must, in my judgment, be recognised by impartial and unprejudiced persons who knew him before he left England in the year 1853. *The evidence that I have had that the plaintiff is my first-born is most positive and conclusive, and it is impossible that I can be mistaken.*

*   *   *

In spite of all this the jury, after no more than half an hour's retirement at the end of this ten months' trial, returned a verdict that the Claimant was guilty of perjury. And because he had sworn on two separate occasions, in a Chancery affidavit and in a trial in the Court of Common Pleas, that he was Roger Tichborne, he got two sentences of seven years—to run consecutively. A fourteen year sentence for such an offence had not been passed since the trial of Titus Oates, whose lies had the distinction of having sent a large number of persons to their deaths. It is very hard to avoid the conclusion that the Claimant had to shoulder the punishment as well as the conscience of society, that he was a curious and unforgettable victim of the hatred we so often feel for those we have wronged. Colour is lent to this conclusion by an extraordinary remark made by Lord Cockburn, the Lord Chief Justice, during the course of the perjury trial. Dr Edward Kenealy, Q.C., counsel for the Claimant, had been dealing with the strange eleventh-hour dicovery of the Tichborne family that Roger Tichborne had a tattooed left arm.

'I shall have no difficulty,' said Kenealy to the jury, 'in proving the tattoo affair a wicked invention.'

The dread prospect at once presented itself that the entire procession of socialites who had gone through the witness-box to swear that Roger Tichborne was tattooed might, in their turn, have to be charged with perjury. Kenealy must be stopped.

'Remember, Dr Kenealy,' said the Lord Chief Justice, 'the moral influence that the conviction of these high person-ages would have upon the country.'

'Moral influence, my Lord,' replied Kenealy, 'is not to be considered in a criminal court.'

But considered it apparently was, at least by the jury, and considered it must have been by the Judges who decided upon the sentence of fourteen years. Mr Justice Mellor, who actually pronounced sentence, said that a fourteen-year imprisonment was 'quite inadequate to the gravity of the offence of which you have been convicted,' although this must have been the reason for giving the Claimant seven years on each count and adding them up. On such a reckoning the law was being very lenient with him. He had sworn dozens of affidavits, obtained large sums of money by pretending that he was Roger Tichborne, committed a felonious forgery every time he signed himself Tichborne through all the years of his 'imposture.' It was, on such a reckoning, lucky for him (rather than the injustice it has always seemed) that as the law then stood he was debarred from giving evidence on his own behalf. Twenty-four years later, the Criminal Evidence Act, 1898, would have given him that right—and allowed him to tell countless lies on oath in open court. With a seven-year penalty for each of them he could have got a total sentence that would make even an American Court seem timid and preoccupied with the present.

There was the same evidence of extraordinary vindictiveness in the attitude of the authorities to the Claimant between the two trials. When his claim had collapsed in the Court of Common Pleas, he was committed to Newgate Prison on a charge of perjury, there to await his indictment and trial. After two months there as an unconvicted prisoner he was released on £5,000 bail, the money being put up by Lord Rivers, Mr Guildford Onslow, M.P. (uncle of the Earl of Onslow,) Dr William Atwood, and Mr James Lamont, all publicly respected figures who had no doubt whatever that the Claimant was Roger Tichborne. A whole year went by; and because Lady Tichborne, his one friend within the gates, had died before the trial, he was bereft of the allowance she had been giving him and the progress of the year's wait reduced him and his family to complete poverty. It also killed off some of his best witnesses.

Not unnaturally, therefore, he decided to appeal to the

public for financial aid, and for that purpose his friends and
supporters convened a succession of public meetings
throughout the United Kingdom. The money began to
come in quite satisfactorily, but, more significantly, growing
public sympathy for his cause was aroused. The Tichborne
family resorted to the law of Contempt of Court, their
first two victims being Guildford Onslow, M.P. and G. H.
Whalley, M.P., who were fined £100 each, plus costs, for
maintaining at a public meeting that the Claimant was
Roger Tichborne when that precise matter was *sub judice*.
G. H. Whalley must have been a man of some resilience: a
little later he wrote to the *Daily News* a letter that supported
the story of the Claimant's rescue from the wreck of the
Bella on the famous journey from Rio de Janeiro. This time
the fine went up to £250 and he was sent to prison, again for
'contempt of court,' in publishing matter that might be
prejudicial to the result of the forthcoming trial. Then a
man named H. J. Cochrane wrote an article in the
Cheltenham Chronicle expressing his view that whoever the
Claimant might be, he was not Arthur Orton. This was one
of the things the perjury trial would be about, so Mr
Cochrane was fined £150. The offence of Mr G. B.
Skipworth, barrister-at-law, who was Deputy Lieutenant of
Lincolnshire and perhaps ought to have known better,
earned him a £500 fine and three months' imprisonment:
he took the chair at a large Brighton meeting in the
Claimant's interests, and made a spirited attack on the
integrity and impartiality of Lord Chief Justice Coleridge,
who, he said, was widely known to have made up his mind
about the Claimant before the trial started. Certainly the
fact that the Lord Chief was on the Bench in both trials was
the subject of much legal misgiving at the time, and is still
spoken of as one of the oddest judicial blunders of the days
before the discovery that justice should not merely be done
but be seen to be done.

*   *   *

The Claimant found himself, in fact, in the curious position between his two trials that, in the eyes of the law, he had no personal identity at all. There is no longer much doubt that, whoever he was, he was not Arthur Orton, and if he decided to pretend he was for the time being, and for the sake of peace and quiet, he would once again have been prejudging a matter that was shortly to be tried in a criminal court. Even to call himself John Smith, safe enough for you and me in our quiet and law-abiding lives, might have been risky for him as an alleged attempt to hold up the courts to ridicule. It was worse still to go on calling himself Roger Tichborne, and presumably, since his claim had been tried and rejected, he would be ill-advised even to call himself the Claimant any more. But his temporary, enforced, and frustrating anonymity was brought home to him in a final and, one would have thought, particularly ham-fisted blow from the High Court.

He happened to be a particularly good marksman with a rifle; and as a means of raising money for his defence, the idea occurred to him and his supporters that he might take part in a series of public shooting matches for prize-money. People in those days would flock to the most ingenuous and unexciting public contests; a sixpenny admission fee would bring in a lot of money. Entertainments Tax had not yet been thought of. Sporting enthusiasts began to put up large sums of money for these shooting exhibitions, in which the Claimant took part as Roger Tichborne, knowing of course that apart from his shooting prowess that name still exercised more public appeal than all the bearded ladies and Siamese twins in the country. But the Tichborne family got the matter before the Judges, who ordered that if he took part in any more such contests or meetings in the name of Roger Tichborne he would go back to prison for contempt of court.

Like everyone who has ever examined this fantastically

true story, I like to choose my position among the various theories that could reconcile (though they never finally will) its innumerable contradictions. I incline to the view that the Claimant was indeed Sir Roger Tichborne and that his case represents one of the most disgraceful miscarriages of justice in the history of English law. On this hypothesis, the conduct of the Judges, of the huge retinue of lawyers, and of the hundreds of witnesses who—on both sides—so clearly committed perjury, was quite cynically evil; but as one who has watched the perjury that goes on daily, and all day long, in the Courts of Justice, I have long recognised and would here record that circumstances of extreme emergency can induce the righteous to take a very subjective view of perjury. Perjury can, in fact, seem white or black: white when it appears to serve the cause of 'natural justice' by defeating the merciless and amoral impartiality of truth; black when resorted to by the people on the other side. But from among the monstrous heap of lies that is called the Tichborne Case, one theory was extracted—without so much as a shred of proof but with engaging verisimilitude— by Serjeant Ballantine; and it is this theory that I find the most acceptable.

The Claimant and Arthur Orton, the butcher's son from Wapping, were known and accepted by everyone to have been friends in the Australian Bush. During their Bush days (suggested Serjeant Ballantine) they had a violent quarrel which led to blows and finally to the death of Arthur Orton. The Claimant then buried him secretly in the Bush. It is certain that throughout the trials, and in private conversation everywhere, he preserved the utmost secrecy about the whereabouts of Arthur Orton, merely suggesting once or twice that he might be in some Australian mental home, nameless and unknown. On the Claimant's return to England from Australia, he went straight to the Orton's former house in Wapping, found that they had left it, and enquired in local pubs and shops for the means to trace them. If he

G

were indeed one of the family but was pretending not to be, this was the conduct of a mental defective. But in fact he never made any secret of his interest in the Orton family, and later he paid them numerous sums of money which, if Serjeant Ballantine's theory is correct, could well have been conscience money, but which are not to be explained, in my view, by family affection. A glance at the physical dissimilarities between the two men, which I have set out on page 187, should be enough to separate their identities beyond the most fanciful doubt; but if that were not enough there would still remain Arthur Orton's known uncouthness of personality and relative illiteracy to be set off against the Claimant's outstanding skill at chess, his eloquence as a public speaker, his skill as an artist and caricaturist, his love and knowledge of music, his famous prowess with the rifle, his skill in the difficult sport of fly-fishing, and his second-nature knowledge of the geography of Paris (his birthplace), of which Orton knew nothing.

If you want to see the enigma of personal identity come to life as a force that can cleave a community into two furious armies, you should try working up a plausible claim to some great estate, while there are still a few left, and serve some writs. Whether it smoulders out in a solicitor's office, over a cheque for hush money, or develops (as it can) into a civil war, the first casualty will be truth and the protagonist will be Justice, hitting and slashing out wildly in the dark and making an example of somebody.

XII

OCULAR PROOF

'**O**CULAR proof' was a kind of Holy Grail to angry, fearful, jealous, or covetous men long before many of them could read, write, or keep files and records about each other. One of the few Shakespearian passages that almost every Othello shouts like a stentor is a demand for visible confirmation of something he doesn't really want to know:

> Villain, be sure thou prove my love a whore—
> Be sure of it; give me the ocular proof;
> Or, by the worth of man's eternal soul
> Thou hadst been better have been born a dog
> Than answer my waked wrath!

In matters of personal identity, we can prove a lot nowadays by seeking out the registrations of births, marriages and deaths; but what is really surprising is how much is left unproven by a certificate of birth, marriage or death, and how very much the evidential value of these documents depends on the convenient circumstance that no one thinks of challenging them. A birth certificate is a copy of an entry made in a register of births, purporting to show when and where a child was born, its name and sex, the names of the parents (including a married mother's maiden name), the father's job, and the signature of the person giving all this information to the Registrar. Any one of those particulars might be false, whether by accident or design, for no attempt is made by anybody to check any of them. Moreover, anyone can walk into the General Register Office at Somerset House, put down the appropriate fee of a few shillings for the necessary search through the Indexes to the registers, and obtain a birth certificate relating to anyone else born in England or Wales at any time since births were first registered. A man who wants to adopt another identity will need to be a little careful: they will ask him at Somerset House to give enough particulars of the birth he is supposed to be looking for to make the search reasonably possible, but even that requirement is an elastic one, and the Register Office officials are an obliging body of men.

If a John Smith, or (more probably) a Mary Jones wants to be taken as of different age from that which the mere march of time allows, nothing is easier than to find in the Indexes an entry in that name to fit the age required. It will be obvious that this kind of deceit can succeed only so long as the people to whom the birth certificate is likely to be produced are people with no knowledge of the other details that it ought to contain—place of birth, parents' names, and so forth; and, as I mentioned in Chapter I, the felony known as 'personation' still carries a maximum penalty of imprisonment for life. The risk is occasionally taken.

About forty years ago a Brentford man left his wife and went to live with another woman. After some years he decided that it was possible to bring about an alteration in the marriage certificate that bound him to his genuine wife, getting his new partner's name substituted for hers and thus providing both women with 'marriage lines,' without the expense and danger of committing bigamy. He went to Somerset House and made out an application for a correction of the entry. How did it come to be wrong, he was asked? He explained that, for reasons that are not relevant here, entirely false information had been given about his wife's name and age at the time of the marriage. When the present registry clerk asked him for some evidence in the shape of a certificate or particulars of his wife's birth, he was unable (as many of us are) to produce a certificate, but he gave full particulars about the birth of the lady he was living with. The marriage registration was accordingly turned up and altered.

Not long afterwards the lawful wife petitioned for divorce, a process that necessitated the production in Court of evidence of the marriage. One can imagine the tragi-comedy that followed the discovery that the real wife's maiden name, age, and place of residence before marriage had all been changed. The case led to some tightening-up of the procedure for making any important correction in marriage entries, especially where the actual identity of one of the parties is involved. I tell the story without anxiety, for you couldn't do it now.

In order to qualify for an inheritance (and this, today, seems to be widely regarded as the supreme function of personal identity) a child must be born alive, but it need live only for an instant of time; and the evidence of the doctor who attended the birth is therefore as vital in such cases as it is in the case of a woman charged with infanticide. Even a child that is born dead has had a provable personal identity between the moment of its conception and the moment before its issue as a lifeless body. In its mother's womb, in its earliest stages as a fœtus, it may have acquired rights and property. If it is born dead it loses them—and they cannot pass through such a child to others.

But dates of birth matter increasingly as the inherent importance of personal identity increases with social benefits. Identification and the tracing of individuals becomes an ever greater industry, and the moment at which some individuals 'come of age' has to be established with painstaking accuracy. By way of example, once the age at which a person can vote in an election is fixed by law, a very close election result may lead to a demand that a particular voter's age qualification be investigated.

Lest it be thought, however, that an entry of birth at a registrar's office is evidence of a human being's existence, it may be as well to recall that, during the last war, the population went up by some fictitious thousands at the instance of people who wanted extra clothing and food coupons. Now that every birth has to be notified to a Medical Officer of Health within thirty-six hours, and every household may at any time receive a solicitous visit from a health visitor, registering imaginary babies is risky. But it is known that some nomadic adventurers actually got extra coupons in this way, and the fact seems to prove three things: first, the tightly-organised welfare State will always produce its own species of small crooks; secondly, a registrar of births can only record what you tell him and has no way of checking it; and (ergo) a birth certificate proves virtually nothing.

But sometimes a birth certificate and a marriage certificate combine to form rather more powerful evidence of identity. In December, 1921, a well-to-do widow named Cecilia Lucy Stollery died, leaving no will and no children. No next-of-kin relatives came forward to claim her quite considerable property, and the Crown therefore stepped in and took it. Three years later three members of a branch of the Stollery family that was surnamed Weir (Reuben, Ann and Joseph) announced that they were the late Mrs Stollery's cousins and applied for letters of administration (they were rather lucky that there was any estate left to administer). Mr Justice Romer held the enquiry in Chambers, and at this enquiry Mrs Stollery was identified as the daughter of a John Brown and Lucy Elizabeth Brown (maiden name Weir). A certificate of her birth in 1857 was produced, and it said that she was Mary Ann Brown; but no one could find the marriage certificate of her parents' marriage.

This is a fairly common occurrence at the General Register Office at Somerset House, and justifies a digression on the subject of illegitimacy, which seems to have an almost magical effect upon the very quality of personal identity. People going to Somerset House in order to establish their origins are found to respond in a variety of ways to the discovery that their own parents were not married. Some appear almost indifferent; some go away thinking with a new indulgence about their parents; some are deeply shocked, either at their parents' morality or at the possible effect of illegitimacy upon their own situations, or at both. Indeed, a distressingly large and bewildered number confide to the Somerset House officials (a humane body of men and women) that their new status is bound to mean chaos in their lives. There are employments that still reject people born out of wedlock—among them, surprisingly enough, being the nursing profession, at least as represented by numerous hospital matrons. It seems that some positive change of identity must be considered to occur in the case of a young probationer nurse who arrives at Somerset House full of enthusiasm and aptitude for the profession she is about to enter and then discovers that her parents have improvidently closed it to her by omitting to get married. I even know of a case in which a young woman, who was an official of a voluntary society for the *protection* of illegitimate children, had occasion to investigate her own origins at Somerset House and discovered that she was illegitimate. 'I must keep that dark,' she said to the Registry Official. 'It wouldn't do for my chairman or the committee to know.' But surely, protested the clerk, she was in the one job where illegitimacy could hardly matter less? On the contrary, it could hardly matter more, she told him: if the fact got known she would be out of a job. It is also interesting that the purpose of the 'shortened form' of birth certificate introduced a few years ago, which conceals illegitimacy, can be simply defeated by the very fact (see page 196) that anyone, including a prospective employer, can obtain anyone else's *full* certificate on application at

Somerset House. It is fairly commonly done, and why it is
done is too obvious to need further discussion.

Illegitimacy, in fact, is universally condemned because
the failure to condemn it would be universally regarded as
an admission that marriage had no special significance. And
since marriage, as a regulated relationship between the
sexes, is in the interests of social order, illegitimacy will
always be with us, destroying happiness, maiming personality and obscuring personal identity.

To return, however, to the story of Mrs Stollery's intestacy,
and the desire of the Weir family to prove that she was Mary
Ann Brown, the daughter of Lucy Elizabeth Brown, née
Weir. Support for this was soon forthcoming in the shape
of Mrs Stollery's birth certificate and those of a brother and
sister, each showing the mother's maiden name as Weir. Unfortunately there was also evidence that the mother's
husband had died, that she had then married a man named
Atkins, and that the certificate of the latter marriage *said she
was then a spinster*. And Mr Justice Romer decided that,
although the certificates afforded evidence of the births of
the people they named, that was all they did; they could
not be considered at all as evidence that the parents were
married. Not unnaturally, the Weirs took this problem to
the Court of Appeal.

This is what Section 38 of the Births and Deaths
Registration Act, 1936, had to say.

All certified copies of entries purporting to be sealed or
stamped with the seal of the said registry office *shall be
received as evidence* of the birth, death, or marriage to
which the same relate, without any further or other proof
of such entry.

But could they be evidence, also, as to the reliability and
accuracy of each other? Was a birth or death certificate
evidence as to the identity of the *parents* of the person who

had just been born or had just died? Or, to put the question in the form it took in the Court of Appeal:

> Were the certified copies of entries in a register of births, deaths, and marriages *prima facie,* or any, evidence of the lawful marriage of John Brown and Lucy Elizabeth Weir?

The Court of Appeal thought it would be rather alarming if Mr Justice Romer's decision were allowed to stand un-altered. Lord Justice Scrutton said that 'in the absence of any special statutory provision, those particulars in the certi-ficate which it was the statutory duty of the registrar to enquire into and learn . . . are evidence. They are admissible evidence, although subject to contradiction by other evidence, of the facts therein stated.' And he went on to point out what would be an important consequence of holding otherwise:

> In no cases (he said) are the rules of evidence applied so strictly as in criminal cases. In several criminal statutes the question whether a crime has been committed or not depends upon the age of the child. As I know from my six years' experience in the criminal courts, it has been the constant practice to admit the certificate as evidence of the date of birth, subject to evidence identifying the particular child against whom* the crime has been com-mitted. If the certificate is not evidence of the date of birth, *all these people have been wrongly convicted . . .* The decision of the learned Judge obviously went too far in saying that the certificates are not, and cannot be, any evidence of a lawful marriage. They may be, in conjunc-tion with other evidence; but whether they are or not will be a question for the master to determine at the enquiry.

But Lord Justice Sargent went nearer to the heart of the matter. 'It does not seem to me,' he said , 'that every part

---

* And he might have added 'or the person by whom'.

of the entry in the register is necessarily of equal weight, as evidence, with every other part of the entry. The whole is admissible as evidence, but it may very well be that with regard to one part there is a greater certainty than with regard to another part. For instance, the date of registration practically *must* be assumed to be conclusive. On the other hand, with regard to the date of the birth, there may be some mistake. *The registrar is acting only on the information of other persons,* with regard to the description of persons, or the place of abode, or matters of that kind, and it may well be that the weight of the evidence varies.'

It was odd that this official exposure of the registrar's certificate, as extremely questionable evidence of identity, should have had to wait until 1921. Within a few years of the passing of the 1836 Registration Act, personation as a criminal source of income was in full swing, and 'adopted' birth certificates were its most popular weapon. For some reason, the Common Law indictment for 'personation,' punishable as a 'cheat' with two years' imprisonment, was seldom if ever resorted to by the prosecuting authorities; but the storm over the fourteen-year perjury sentence on the Tichborne Claimant in 1874 (see Chapter XI) brought the whole question of personation into discussion and resulted in the passing of the False Personation Act, 1874, the main provision of which was as follows:

If any person shall falsely and deceitfully personate any person, or the heir, executor, or administrator, wife, widow, next-of-kin, or relation of any person, with intent fraudulently to obtain any land, estate, chattel, money, valuable security or property, he shall be guilty of felony and upon conviction shall be liable to imprisonment for life.

However, prosecutions under this Act were but little more frequent than those that had been based on the Common

Law; and in the last half-century the temptation to personate the heirs to the few worth-while properties that remain has been powerfully mitigated by the hovering obligation to present half the proceeds to the National Trust and pay over the other half in death duties.

In the last resort, identity will never be capable of absolute proof by related documents, whether they are birth or marriage certificates, passports, specimens of handwriting, identity cards, or (such is the skill of the forger) compulsorily-registered finger prints. This dignity of personal identity can therefore be lost, leaving the loser poor beyond the meaning of words. We have seen that it subsists after death, protecting an ancestor, a memory, an intention, a line of descent, or corpse, even a grave. There are millions who believe that it attaches to the essence or spirit of the legions who have died, so that persons held in affection during life can still be recognised and spoken to across the void. Still very sceptical as to this, the law nevertheless holds that it subsists before birth, so long as conception can be medically proved. There is endless scope for speculation, on lines suggested by the philosophy of 'selfhood,' about the probability that it exists before conception, so that the millions unborn, no less than the millions who have lived and died, have and have always had their millions of inviolable personal identities. In this book I have avoided, in fear and ignorance, these roadless wastes; but the law sometimes shows its awareness of them.

At Westminster County Court on 3rd February, 1946, Judge Blagden explained why, a few weeks before in Chambers, he had made an order that the Registrar-General must disclose the name and address of an adopted girl—one of the few cases in which Somerset House will rigidly withhold information from the curious, 'except under an order of a court of competent jurisdiction.' She had money to come from her grandmother, whose executors had been unable to trace the girl because they did not know her real name. 'The circumstances here,' said the Judge, 'are such that I feel the Court can make the order. But I do it on the terms that the information is to be used solely for the purpose of paying the legacy. In general,' he went on,

> it is the policy of the law to make the veil between the past and present lives of an adopted person as opaque and impenetrable as possible, like the veil which God in His wisdom has placed between the living and the dead. Injudicious attempts to penetrate the latter have caused a great deal of misery. No less tragic results may easily flow from a child tracing its real mother from motives of curiosity, and still more in the case of unscrupulous persons with sinister motives.*

I have not seen, in the law-books or elsewhere, a more compendious judicial reference to the whole mystery of personal identity—the veil, the curiosity, the past and the present, the tragedy, the positive 'I-am-I' assertiveness that has, in general, the blessing of the law.

But the law's conception of identity has to be and remain ideological: although it likes things that it can see, handle, label, measure, and pass round the jury box, the law of identity is essentially made up of ideas, all of which derive from impressions. There is no 'impression' of self, wrote David Hume, and therefore no idea of self. 'For my part,' he said, 'when I enter most intimately into what I call *myself*, I always stumble on some particular conception or other—of heat or cold, light or shade, love or hatred, pain or pleasure. I never catch *myself* at any time without a perception, and never can observe anything but the perception.' And he remarks ironically that there may be some philosophers who can actually perceive their own selves; 'but setting aside some metaphysicians of this kind, I may venture to affirm of the rest of mankind that they are nothing

---

* *Daily Telegraph*, 4th February, 1956.

but a bundle or collection of different perceptions, which succeed each other with inconceivable rapidity and are in a perpetual flux and movement.'* The whole of modern psychological knowledge can, in fact, be stated without introducing the Self; the idea of it can be conveyed in terms of *perceived* things or events, so that by substituting the definition for what it defines you can always make a statement of what you know without the need to bring in any *unperceived* things or events. It doesn't matter to the law that the idea of substance, or body, is thus banished from the psychology of perception and therefore of personal identity. Hume totally abolished the idea of substance from psychology. When Berkeley was supposed to have done the same thing in the case of physics, he encountered (or perhaps he didn't perceive it?) the sonorous sarcasm of Samuel Johnson, who said: 'Pray, Sir, don't leave us; for we may perhaps forget to think of you, and then you will cease to exist.' In this, of course, as in other matters, Dr Johnson may conceivably have been rather an ass. But he would have made a wonderful lawyer; and you can almost call him the patron saint of personal identity.

* *Treatise of Human Nature*, Book I, part iv, section vi.